First Sunday

Spiritual Responses to the 9-11 Attacks

http://FirstSundayBook.com

Edited by

Donald Robert Elton & Aura Agudo Elton

Donald Robert Elton & Aura Agudo Elton

ISBN-13: 978-1460902882

ISBN-10: 1460902882

Copyright © 2011 by Donald R. Elton and Aura A. Elton
All Rights Reserved

First Sunday

Dedication

This book is dedicated to the victims of the 9-11 attacks, the first responders, members of the armed forces defending our nations against terrorism, and the church leaders who help us find comfort, meaning, purpose and hope in these difficult times.

Donald Robert Elton & Aura Agudo Elton

Acknowledgement

This book would not have been possible without the support of the many contributors. Without exception they were enthusiastic in their support. The comments written to accompany their sermons were thoughtful and provided great insight into their objectives in writing great sermons that were written under difficult circumstances and with inspired guidance.

First Sunday

Table of Contents

Introduction 7

President George W. Bush 10

Rev. Timothy C. Ahrens 15

Rev. Scott W. Alexander 28

Rev. George Antonakos 41

Pastor Daniel B. Barker 51

Rev. M. Craig Barnes 60

Rev. David M. Bryce 68

Rev. Benjamin R. Doolittle 85

Rev. Keith Grogg 91

Rev. John Hamby 101

Rev. John A. Huffman, Jr. 110

Pastor Eun-sang Lee 133

Rabbi Ellen Lewis 139

Rev. Keith Linkous 151

Rev. Michael McCartney 159

Pastor Travis Moore 180

Donald Robert Elton & Aura Agudo Elton

Pastor Glenn Newton 189

Rev. Ronald W. Scates...202

Rev. Jim Standiford 213

Rev. Andrew Stirling 225

Rev. Jack Wyman...242

About the Editors...258

First Sunday

Introduction

We all remember historic events that we witnessed during our lifetimes. The Kennedy assassinations, Martin Luther King's assassination, the end of the Viet Nam War, the Apollo 11 moon landing, the Challenger and Columbia accidents, and now the September 11, 2001, terrorist attacks against the United States. These are all events that divide our lives into chapters.

That Tuesday morning I was making hospital rounds and noticed all the TV's were showing the same images. Soon it became apparent that this was not a simple though dramatic plane crash. Everyone was quiet and hospital patients, employees, doctors, and visitors all gathered around TV's throughout the hospital. Later in the morning we brought in a TV at the office as well to follow the events as they unfolded. Not much work got done – nothing else seemed very important that morning and on into the days that followed.

Aura had just arrived in the United States just three days before 9-11 to start a new life. She had been a US Citizen through marriage since 1992, while living in Panama around the Canal Zone. This was a time of great transition for her and to arrive on the mainland just in time to witness the events of 9-11 was quite a shock. Through the sorrow and tragedy of those days, she, like many people around the world, for the first time really felt what it was to be an American.

Donald Robert Elton & Aura Agudo Elton

People were confused, some afraid, some angry, but all were mesmerized by the horrible historic events that occurred, and all were asking who was responsible? Why did they do this? How could they do this? Perhaps most important: Were they done?

Many headed to Church that Sunday and the Sundays that followed hoping for comfort and for explanations how God could allow this to happen to a country founded on the principles of freedom of religion and expression. How could this happen to so many people, none of whom could have possibly done anything to inspire such an attack? These were civilians doing what we all do every day, going to work in offices, traveling for business or pleasure, and just generally living their lives. This event served to remind us that when we leave our homes in the morning we never really can know how the day will end for us.

Last year we were visiting Washington, DC on business and I wanted to show my wife Ford's Theatre where Abraham Lincoln was watching a play only to be assassinated by John Wilkes Booth, a prominent actor well known in Washington. While in the gift shop we ran across a book titled:

We Saw Lincoln Shot: One Hundred Eyewitness Accounts, by Timothy Good, University Press of Mississippi, Jackson, MS, 1995, ISBN 0878057781.

First Sunday

We wanted to do something similar regarding the 9-11 attacks but there were so many witnesses around the world that just giving the eye witness accounts wouldn't have much meaning perhaps for a century or more. We then decided to start looking around at church sermons given shortly after the attacks as we had both heard a few that were particularly inspirational. We felt this would be a valuable project to put together a compilation of uplifting and inspirational sermons that would bring people back in time to where they were and how they felt 10 years ago during and after the terrorist attacks. Many of these are difficult to read without revisiting the emotions of those tense days. Ten years later it is more important than ever to remember what happened, who we were, and who we are today.

As for the sermons, remember that most of these were written on very short notice by people who were themselves deeply moved and affected by the events that had just occurred. Much information about the events such as casualty counts, perpetrators, and other details were not yet known when these were written. The fact that so many of these sermon's are so moving written under the pressures of time and the events themselves makes them even more amazing. Ten years later and beyond, these words will, we believe, continue to awaken thoughts and feelings perhaps pushed aside as life goes on.

Don & Aura

Donald Robert Elton & Aura Agudo Elton

President George W. Bush
43rd President of the United States
National Cathedral
Washington, DC

Friday, September 14, 2001

Remarks at the National Day of Prayer and Remembrance Service

We are here in the middle hour of our grief. So many have suffered so great a loss, and today we express our Nation's sorrow. We come before God to pray for the missing and the dead and for those who love them.

On Tuesday our country was attacked with deliberate and massive cruelty. We have seen the images of fire and ashes and bent steel. Now come the names, the list of casualties we are only beginning to read.

They are the names of men and women who began their day at a desk or in an airport, busy with life. They are the names of people who faced death and in their last moments called home to say, "Be brave," and, "I love you." They are the names of passengers who defied their murderers and prevented the murder of others on the ground. They are the names of men and women who wore the uniform of the United States and died at their posts. They are the names of rescuers, the ones whom death found running up the stairs and into the fires to help others. We will read all these

First Sunday

names. We will linger over them and learn their stories, and many Americans will weep.

To the children and parents and spouses and families and friends of the lost, we offer the deepest sympathy of the Nation. And I assure you, you are not alone.

Just 3 days removed from these events, Americans do not yet have the distance of history. But our responsibility to history is already clear: To answer these attacks and rid the world of evil.
War has been waged against us by stealth and deceit and murder. This Nation is peaceful, but fierce when stirred to anger. This conflict was begun on the timing and terms of others. It will end in a way and at an hour of our choosing.

Our purpose as a nation is firm. Yet, our wounds as a people are recent and unhealed and lead us to pray. In many of our prayers this week, there is a searching and an honesty. At St. Patrick's Cathedral in New York on Tuesday, a woman said, "I prayed to God to give us a sign that He is still here." Others have prayed for the same, searching hospital to hospital, carrying pictures of those still missing.
God's signs are not always the ones we look for. We learn in tragedy that his purposes are not always our own. Yet, the prayers of private suffering, whether in our homes or in this great cathedral, are known and heard and understood.

Donald Robert Elton & Aura Agudo Elton

There are prayers that help us last through the day or endure the night. There are prayers of friends and strangers that give us strength for the journey. And there are prayers that yield our will to a will greater than our own.

This world He created is of moral design. Grief and tragedy and hatred are only for a time. Goodness, remembrance, and love have no end. And the Lord of life holds all who die and all who mourn.

It is said that adversity introduces us to ourselves. This is true of a nation as well. In this trial, we have been reminded, and the world has seen, that our fellow Americans are generous and kind, resourceful and brave. We see our national character in rescuers working past exhaustion, in long lines of blood donors, in thousands of citizens who have asked to work and serve in any way possible.

And we have seen our national character in eloquent acts of sacrifice. Inside the World Trade Center, one man, who could have saved himself, stayed until the end at the side of his quadriplegic friend. A beloved priest died giving the last rites to a firefighter. Two office workers, finding a disabled stranger, carried her down 68 floors to safety. A group of men drove through the night from Dallas to Washington to bring skin grafts for burn victims.

First Sunday

In these acts, and in many others, Americans showed a deep commitment to one another and an abiding love for our country. Today we feel what Franklin Roosevelt called the warm courage of national unity. This is a unity of every faith and every background. It has joined together political parties in both Houses of Congress. It is evident in services of prayer and candlelight vigils and American flags, which are displayed in pride and wave in defiance.

Our unity is a kinship of grief and a steadfast resolve to prevail against our enemies. And this unity against terror is now extending across the world.

America is a nation full of good fortune, with so much to be grateful for. But we are not spared from suffering. In every generation, the world has produced enemies of human freedom. They have attacked America because we are freedom's home and defender. And the commitment of our fathers is now the calling of our time.

On this National Day of Prayer and Remembrance, we ask Almighty God to watch over our Nation and grant us patience and resolve in all that is to come. We pray that He will comfort and console those who now walk in sorrow. We thank Him for each life we now must mourn and the promise of a life to come.

As we have been assured, neither death nor life, nor angels nor principalities nor powers, nor things present nor things to come, nor height nor depth, can separate us from God's love. May He bless the souls of the departed. May He comfort our own, and may He always guide our country.

God bless America.

First Sunday

Rev. Timothy C. Ahrens

The First Congregational Church, United Church of Christ Columbus, Ohio

Sunday, September 16, 2001

September 11, 2001, is a day whose events are emblazoned in my mind and spirit. The horror and the heroes, the images and the impact have shaped us in ways we may never fully realize. My relationships in the past ten years have grown to meaningfully include many Muslims, Jews, Christians, and secular people whom I may never have known if the planes in New York, Washington, and Shanksville, PA had not destroyed thousands of lives and shattered and shaped our nation's view of itself in the world in which we live.

On September 12, 2001 the city of Columbus gathered in an interfaith service in our sanctuary. More than one thousand people came downtown that night to worship with people of all faiths and no faith at all. They came to weep and hold on to each other. While a deep sense of the evil which had struck at the heart of our the world 30+ hours before was present, an even deeper sense of the light of God shone in the hearts of the 1,000 people gathered in our sanctuary that night. It is a moment of sheer epiphany as God's light overcame evil once again! By the time I delivered the sermon you see in this book, I was centered in a new understanding and a new focus on the future and the power of God to prevail over evil. This past summer, I lived, worshiped and prayed among Jews, Christians and Muslims in Spain, Israel, the Palestinian territories and Egypt. I offered a daily blog about this experience through <u>The Columbus Dispatch.</u> *As "Children of Abraham" we need to find a way out of the madness of violence and into a pathway of peace and justice. We must do this together. It will only come as we worship, pray, and break bread with one another. I experienced the change of hearts in my singular journey - a journey of faith deeply touched and shaped by the events of September 11, 2001.*

Play the Ball Where the Monkey Drops It!

I Corinthians 15:51-58; Matthew 19:13-15
As I look out at you this morning, you can't even imagine how I feel at this moment. As I look out on you, I am deeply grateful to our Glorious God for this moment in time. I am thankful this morning and in this moment for each and every one of you. I am thankful that you are alive!
I am thankful for your presence here in worship today.

Let us pray.

First Sunday

May the words of my mouth and meditations of each one of our hearts be acceptable in your sight, O Lord, our strength and our salvation. Amen.

Please listen to this parable . . .
Apparently, not long after the British colonized India, a deep yearning for recreation led them to build the Tollygunge Golf course in Calcutta. However, golf in Calcutta presented peculiar hazards. Monkeys would drop out of trees, scurry around the course and seize the golf balls. They would play with the balls, tossing them here, there and everywhere. Monkeys did not fit into anyone's understanding of golf!

At first the golfers tried to contain the monkeys. Their strategy was to build high fences around the fairways and greens. However, you can imagine - fences presented no real challenge to monkeys. Soon, the fences came down. Next, the golfers tried to lure the monkeys away from the course. However, the monkeys found nothing more entertaining than watching humans go wild when their balls were disturbed - so they didn't leave. Then the golfers tried trapping the monkeys and carrying them away. But, for every monkey that was caught, another would appear. Finally, the golfers gave in to the monkeys and tried a novel approach - play the ball where the monkey drops it.

As you can imagine, playing this way could be rather maddening. For example, the ball is driven well down the fairway close to the hole - only to have the monkey run off with it and drop it somewhere far from the hole. On the other hand, the opposite sometimes happened. A terrible shot might be picked up and delivered close to the cup. It didn't take long before golfers realized that golf on that particular course was quite similar to our experience of life - there are good breaks and there are bad breaks and we cannot entirely control the outcome of the game called life. Like it or not, Life is all about playing the ball where the monkey drops it.

When I came across this story some months ago, I thought of today and our commissioning of Dorinda White into the Ministry of Christian Education. CE work is much like this: you play the ball where the monkey drops it. There are many uncontrolled elements of the work. A parent comes to you in tears about struggles they are having with one of their classes or children; a child has a particularly bad day; or on the other hand, a child or teen has a tremendous breakthrough in their journey! In these times, I have seen Dorinda lead people through to the other side of the experience - especially sorting out the good in the presence of what appears only to be bad.

Needless to say, on Tuesday, 9-11, the monkey dropped the ball in the worst possible place in all of our collective memories. For a day or two, the staff wondered if we should even proceed with this celebration today. In the end, we all decided we needed to celebrate the good news

First Sunday

of Christ's power and presence in the educational ministry of First Church and in Dorinda's gifts for this ministry. I felt God calling us not to flee in the face of evil and the horrors of this past week, but to move forward in faith together. But, before moving toward this great celebration, please allow me to share some thoughts and prayers concerning the tragedy of this past week.

"Play the Ball Where the Monkey Drops It!"

On Tuesday, September 11, yes - 9-11, between 8:00-11:00 am, terrorists in four places, in four commercial airplanes, perpetrated unprecedented acts of war and evil upon the citizens of the United States of America and the world. Acts of war - yes! But, I know that some of my ministerial colleagues choose not to name Tuesday's actions as "evil." While I respect them greatly for their thoughts, they believe that to name such actions as evil will add to inciting our government and our citizens to strike out in similar actions against men and women and children somewhere else on the globe.

However, I believe what happened was nothing short of evil. And it was also a choice for evil! It was done by those whose hearts and minds were consumed by hate and by evil. Evil is defined as "morally wrong, wicked, harmful, injurious and depraved, vicious, corrupt, vile, and nefarious." To turn four commercial airliners loaded with civilians and tremendous volume of fuel against centers of commerce in the height of daily work and against the center of military planning is EVIL.

Now, the danger of dealing with such evil is that it pervades the human heart and mind. In response, we must not be drawn into actions as persons or as a nation which call forth darkness and evil of our own inclinations and perpetrations! In Paul's words, "Overcome evil with good."

And we must never assume that because we, as Americans, are the reacting strike force, that what we do and how we do it is good in and of itself. Children and innocents abroad must not die in retribution for the death of innocents and children in our native land!

As the Jewish year comes to an end and reading from the Torah focus on the last passages from the fifth and final book of Torah, Deuteronomy 34, we are reminded that God calls Moses and all of us to make choices - for after all - life is about making choices. God tells Moses to choose good over evil; to choose blessings not curses; to choose life, not death.

In a moment we will look at our choices for good, for life, for blessings. But, first I need to tell you that what we all witnessed Tuesday was what I named it to be on the cover of the First Church News (which was written as buildings were being attacked and falling)!.

First Sunday

Tuesday was the single worst day of loss on American soil in the 225 years of our nation's history! It appears that well over 6,000 people are dead or missing at this point. Outside of losses numbering close to 6,000 people in a hurricane which struck Galveston, Texas in 1990 and the single day loss of over 4,000 soldiers from North and South at Antietam in 1862, our country has never lost so many lives on American soil in one day in over 82,200 days of our existence as a nation. During the American Revolution, fought between 1775-1783, we did not lose as many lives as we lost Tuesday! Comparisons have been made to the Japanese attack on Pearl Harbor. On that day, 2,800 soldiers and civilians were killed in a military action against a military base. I fact on pearl Harbor, not to suggest that the horrors of one experience override the horrors of the other. Rather, I share this to say that as we feel the total impact of this huge devastation, we are right to feel that this may be the worst single day in American history! (For example, as horrid as the bombing of the Federal Building in Oklahoma City was, 168 lives were taken in that terrorist action.) To feel overwhelmingly numb, shocked, angry, everything else is perfectly understandable considering the hugeness of this devastation. As Bob Scheffer of ABC News said Thursday night, "The more I look at the rubble of the WTC, the larger and the worse it becomes."

Donald Robert Elton & Aura Agudo Elton

As this drama has been unfolding, we have all been given strength by the stories of people rallying to support the fallen and the valiant men and women working the rescue missions on Manhattan's lower east side and at the Pentagon. THESE ARE ALL STORIES ABOUT PEOPLE CHOOSING LIFE!

The Firefighters, police, EMS of NYC stand tall - and thousands of stories of volunteers, reserves and active duty military, medical personnel continue to amaze us and inspire us.

In addition, I was reminded by Bob Woods, a Delta pilot and F-16 fighter pilot in the reserves, we must never forget the heroes of Flight 93 which crashed in Somerset, Pennsylvania. He said, "As airlines' pilots we are trained to deal with terrorists based on our knowledge of the last experience. We must all remember that the most recent, last experience of airborne terrorists was Flight 93 - not the other three flights. On that flight, the men and women passengers courageously battled the terrorists and sacrificed their own lives to save the lives of thousands of others on the ground. That battle in the airspace over Ohio and Pennsylvania is the last experience on which all the new training models will be based." Following those words, Bob Woods and Mike Ponzoni and other pilots - members and close friends of this congregation - courageously took off to do their jobs!

First Sunday

We must all thank God, and thank the heroes and angels of mercy from this past week who saved literally thousands of lives by their calm demeanor and valiant actions on behalf of people they did not know.

We must remember who we are and to whom we belong. We must act with love and justice on behalf of others We must choose to act against injustice and to act with mercy.

We are children of a living God! We belong to God in Jesus Christ our Lord! Here at First Church, we have entered into a study course in Christian Education entitled, "Who is my neighbor?" In facing the horrors of this day - we must name and embrace Arab and Muslim Americans are our neighbors. We are being abandoned by most of the Islamic world because of the actions of these days.

On Wednesday night, as worshipers were coming out of Ascension Lutheran Church, they were greeted by Somali-American Muslims who lined the sidewalks in solidarity with their sisters and brothers from another faith. In the First Church family, we have relatives and friends who are Islamic and of Middle Eastern descent. Some of them may be Arabic. They are facing renewed prejudice and hatred in these days. We need to reach out to them and hold on to them!

ABC News carried a story about a woman in Oregon - a 30 year old Palestinian-American citizen - who was facing hate in her community because she owned and operated an Arabic language school. In the piece, it was also pointed out that she was a Christian. OSU President Brit Kirwan (and a member of First Church) spoke passionately on Wednesday about stopping hate crimes or hateful words or actions against persons in out community who may be of Middle Eastern or Islamic background. It was a moving statement of truth and sanity. Make sure your Islamic and Arabic friends, family, and neighbors are okay. Find out how you can help them and support them this week.

We must also take care of each other. We must choose to love!

As the shock wears off the full range of emotions will come out. I have found myself highly emotional in all sorts of situations this week. I know that you have been, too. Please, be gentle with your children and spouses and loved ones and coworkers. NONE OF US HAS CAUSED THIS. Let's not take out our feelings on other people. Talk to people, express yourself. Find healthy outlets for your emotions. I have always found it to be true that when my feelings don't come out in healthy ways, like toxic waste, they will seep out in unhealthy ways. Turn the terror and fear and hurt you are feeling to love. Hold your loved ones longer and closer. Ask for hugs if you need them. Practice random acts of kindness for those who are isolated, shut-in, homebound. They are all alone in their fears and feelings this week. Take some flowers to the nearest

First Sunday

Firehouse or Police station or to a pilot or flight attendant you know - they have all lost brothers and sisters in this battle this week. Ask at work and school if people have experienced personal loss in this tragedy. Take care of yourself, too. Take a walk. Breathe deeper. Write letters to Congress and the President. Express your feelings so they don't turn into toxins within your soul. And help those closest to you, especially children to express themselves, too.

We must also make the choice for God to guide us! We need to seek in prayer and daily direction for God to guide us as individuals and as a community in the midst of this crisis and tragedy.

Many of us have given blood. Many have shared donations. Today, in a moment we will share in a special offering for Church World Service for the relief efforts in NYC and Washington, D.C. Mary Ann Goetz called me and asked if the children could use pint containers and collect "pints of pennies" since they can't give blood. Great idea. I called Fifth Avenue Presbyterian Church, Dr. Tom Tewell on Thursday and asked what we can do to help. "Pray unceasingly!" said Tom's secretary. I suggested we might send childcare workers to them when the memorial services begin, so that their members can worship and know their kids are loved and cared for by brother and sisters in Christ. This region's head of Church World Service told me one of their greatest needs is for grief counselors right now. Could we send professional help to them? If you know a retired counselor or folks who could make the trip, let them know they are needed. The shock is wearing off and people are needed now and in the months (and years ahead)! Let's think outside the box and find ways to reach out to New Yorkers or Capital Area families in need.

Finally, we must clearly and simply choose God! Our God reigns! God is in control!

Paul writes in Romans 12, "Neither death, nor life, nor principalities, nor powers, nothing else in all creation can separate us from the love of God in Christ Jesus our Lord." God is in the midst of all of this - calling us to stand in solidarity with our American sisters and brothers in needs and our global family in its time of grieving, too.

My prayer is that this brings those who seek life, and good closer together. I know God has brought us together this day for purposes beyond our creating! God has brought us together to love one another. God has brought us together to hold on to one another. God has brought us together to mend the broken hearts of one another. God has brought us together to mourn the horrific losses of this week. For Jesus Says, "The blessed ones who mourn shall be comforted." God has brought us together to be merciful in this day and in the days ahead. For Jesus Says, "The blessed ones who are merciful shall receive mercy." God

First Sunday

has brought us together to be molded and shaped as peacemakers. For Jesus says, " The blessed ones, the peacemakers shall be called children of God!" God had brought us together to praise His Holy and Everlasting Name! So, our prayer is for God to bless us in this time. Now, let us pause from grieving and reflecting to see that the ball has been dropped close to the cup. Let us celebrate God's glorious love in the sharing our morning offering for Church World Service and the commissioning of Dorinda White in our Ministry of Christian Education.

And please know, from the depths of my heart, I love you! I love each and every one of you! And never forget - God loves you. May God bless you and your loved ones - now and always!

Amen.

Donald Robert Elton & Aura Agudo Elton

Rev. Scott W. Alexander

River Road Unitarian Church
Bethesda, Maryland

Sunday, September 16, 2001

Sermon preparation that week was extremely difficult and emotional. Our church is located just a few miles from the pentagon where one of the planes crashed, many folks were traumatized by the attack, and many had to walk miles home that day because of subway fears. I wanted to offer just the right mixture of reassurance and challenge, and I rewrote my material many times, waking up in the middle of the night several nights with changes and rewrites.

That Sunday was highly emotional, with both services absolutely packed to the ceiling. Both my Associate Minister and I preached, and between the two of us we seemed to touch just the right notes, as countless listeners thanked us profusely for ministering to them. Several visitors reported that that Sunday was the day they realized they had found a church home. People felt empowered to move on in a positive, compassionate, and brave ways.

I am gratified that everything I said on that Sunday 9 years ago still rings true to me today. I believe I touched on all the right themes in my sermon that first Sunday after 9-11, themes which have as much importance today for

First Sunday

humanity as they did then. Our world remains a very troubled, divided, violent place, and all people of faith and goodwill need to rise above the brutality of what is, as they work to build the better, more just world that still can be.

WHAT IS ON OUR HEARTS TODAY

"Dear God, may the words of my mouth and the meditations of my heart be acceptable in thy sight..." What does one say in a house of faith and hope and love...on the Sunday following horrific violence and unfathomable cruelty like that which unfolded before our disbelieving eyes on Tuesday morning?

Emotions come much easier to the throat than words do. Like all of you, I am still personally reeling from the magnitude of the horror, inhumanity and death which was let loose on our nation by these terrorists...and with each passing day I (again, I suspect like all of you) am slowly (and reluctantly, because I am not sure I want to face the incredible complexity and magnitude of all this) realizing how profoundly the events of this week will change all of our lives, for years (if not decades) to come.

Though this crisis has been a long time coming, the world has nonetheless suddenly been turned upside down this week. There is incredible danger and uncertainty ahead for every human being everywhere on this globe...and no one - no one -- should underestimate the impossible complexity and profound unpredictability of what lies ahead. Anyone who imagines that there is any sort of easy or quick fix - military, diplomatic or otherwise - has simply not thought long or deeply enough about the incredibly intricate global dynamics and root causes of this kind of violence and conflict. Like you, I have so many intense thoughts and emotions right now...reactions which seem all tangled up with one another, not unlike the jumbled wreckage which lies in a heap where the proud World Trade Towers once stood. The first thing, then, we must acknowledge out loud this morning is the painful dislocation of being we all feel. The violence of this week has been horrific...we are beginning to realize that there is much more chaos and upheaval to come...and we are all reeling inside from it.

Over the recent days since these violent tragedies -- as I have talked with and listened to you the congregation I serve (and neighbors and friends and family) -- it has become clear to me that we are brought together in this difficult time by a commonality of heart that cuts across all of our many diversities and differences.

First, of course, there is the profound grief and sadness we all have upon our hearts. The grief and sadness we now feel is multidimensional and complex -- beginning with the intense sorrow felt by those among us who have been personally and directly affected by Tuesday's violence - most especially those of you who lost a loved-one, coworker, friend or acquaintance. But our grief does not

First Sunday

stop there. All Americans, whether or not we personally knew any of the (what we now know to be) thousands of victims of this terrible violence, nonetheless share a heart-wrenching and dislocating grief that can also be fiercely personal and emotionally intense. As a national people -- despite all the many diversities of language, culture, race and nationality that make the United States so rich and beautiful ... including the more than 6 million of our Arab-American neighbors - we Americans are powerfully connected to one another by a strong (and generous) web of concern, empathy and compassion that becomes unmistakable when such national tragedies occur. It is right and it is good, then, that Americans grieve for one another (and rush - as we did at every blood bank and house of worship in the country) to offer support for one another. The universal heaviness of heart we have felt (and the connection of being we have expressed to one another) over recent days is a sign that that our nation is strong and compassionate and united...a nation built upon a foundation of respect and concern for one another. The grief we now feel for the suffering of our fellow citizens reminds us of the best which this nation stands for, and calls us to renew and revitalize our care for, and connection with, one another in the difficult days ahead.

And we must also recognize today that some of the grief we feel is grief for ourselves ... for our own sense of lost personal security...for the shattering of some of the innocence and sense of safety we had about our national way of life...and for our children - God bless them all -- who we now know must grow up in an increasingly dangerous world. This kind of grief, too, is appropriate, for much has indeed been lost this week.

So there is much grief upon our hearts this day, and the first step in beginning to positively move with and (eventually) through that multilayered grief is to recognize the full extent of what we are feeling, and affirm its power and its rightness, even as we begin, slowly, to process and manage it ... which we (in time) will.

Secondly, there is (of course) a great deal of fear and apprehension upon our hearts. How can any of us go through events of national violence like the ones of this week and not feel profoundly less safe and personally more vulnerable and helpless than we did before? It has been often observed by psychological professionals that fear is amongst the most primordial and powerful of human emotions. It is natural and universal for us to feel fear when we encounter danger. No one is exempt from it ... and pretending now that we don't have it is neither realistic or healthy. This is a time of palpable fear and apprehension in America. Yes, we can and should offer ourselves and one another many realistic reassurances about the future (and must also do so repeatedly with our children and grandchildren who need our calm and reassuring presence to put their fears in perspective) but we must also -- each of us this week -- fully acknowledge

First Sunday

and face the very real fear we are experiencing. There is no weakness in having fear, only strength. For our fears can (if properly understood and channeled) help us to mobilize our positive human resources to create a better and safer and more just and peaceful world for all. I pray that out of our fears will arise fresh resolve (in each of us) to do what we can -- and there is always something each of us can do...as long as we have breath none of us is powerless -- to bring more goodness, more compassion, more justice and hope to humanity everywhere.

Lying just beyond our fear and apprehension is the third emotion I want to focus on this morning. There is, of course, a great deal of anger and rage in our hearts.

And it is here -- with our anger and rage -- that I want to spend most of my time this morning.

I believe it is terribly important that we deal with these volatile emotions maturely, wisely, and with principle ... always with principle. As American citizens, we are angry -- some of us profoundly and bitterly so. We are angry at the terrorists who planned these cowardly and inhumane attacks. We angry at their shadowy organizations which plan other violent acts. We are angry at any national governments which can be proven to have in any way tolerated, encouraged or supported them. Our anger is, of course, natural and justified. There has been a great loss of innocent life, and we must not pretend (even the most pacifistic and peace-loving amongst us) that we do not feel outrage about what has transpired (and some primordial desire to get back at those who did this). It is perhaps crucial, however, to remind ourselves at this juncture of our national life that our national anger is inextricably interwoven with our fear...and just as (as I have already said this morning) we must not let our fears (and the fears of our children) get out of proportion, we must also not allow our anger to get out perspective, thus causing us to act in impulsive ways that abrogate the very principles and nobility upon which this free republic (and our culture) was built.

Like all of you, over recent days I have been feverishly reading the morning newspaper cover to cover, watching with full heart hours upon hours of heart-wrenching television, and talking (with almost everyone I meet) about the complexities of these terrible events. As a religious leader, I am deeply worried by the hateful vehemence, the blind simplicity, the thoughtless self-righteousness of the anger I am now hearing many Americans expressing. I am deeply concerned that most of our political and military leaders (beginning with our President and key congressional leaders), as well as a vast majority of the American people, seem to be loudly calling for swift vengeance, sweeping military action and sure retribution.

First Sunday

Now please hear that as one American citizen I too want my government to respond resolutely in defense of our people and our way of life.

I want justice to be done, I want safety to be restored across this land, and I understand this will almost certainly necessitate strong military action being taken.

But as a Unitarian Universalist -- long committed to finding peaceful, rational and humane solutions to human conflict whenever and wherever possible...and as an American citizen passionately committed to the our dream of establishing justice, freedom and dignity for all -- I also want my leaders and my nation to move carefully, judiciously, and morally.

I don't want us to lose any more than we already have. I want my government to wisely analyze our entire global situation in all of its numbing complexities (rejecting overly simplistic solutions that seldom work)-and when we do, wisely act, remaining true to our highest principles and most deeply held values. I join with Cardinal Theodore E. McCarrick, archbishop of Washington who cautioned this week at a mass of mourning at St. Matthews,
"We must pray for our leaders that they will not lose sight of the fact that we are a nation of laws. Our response (to this terror) must be strong...and just. And we must not take our anger and anxieties out on a whole nation, a whole people or a whole ethnic group."

Donald Robert Elton & Aura Agudo Elton

I pray with all my heart that our national leaders -- most especially President Bush and his advisors -- move measuredly and morally ... making sure that (after we have established precisely who is responsible for these crimes against humanity, and have thought through the many consequences of every option) whatever our eventual response is in accordance with the highest and most humane principles of our nation.

Again... Americans are rightfully and naturally angry. Terrible crimes against innocent citizens have been committed, and we must and will respond forcefully to try to ensure such horrors never happen again here or anywhere else in the world. But at the same time, I believe with all my heart that our national anger is at least as dangerous to us (and to everything we value) as any terrorists are.

Let me enumerate the dangers I see. First, there is clearly the danger (surely you can all see it)? That an angry and indiscriminate military response could only unwittingly contribute to an unending upward spiral of violence, that would only further jeopardize our world and the possibilities for true justice and lasting peace for all. Second (AND THIS IS VERY IMPORTANT), there is the danger that in any angry and indiscriminate response we will arrogantly oversimplify the terribly complex geopolitical realities and forces (which we have actively participated in as a dominant nation, not always with

First Sunday

absolute innocence and justice) that have gotten us to this international crisis point. For example, I quote the global strategic analysts Daniel Benjamin and Steven Simon, who wisely wrote this week that this terrorism just didn't spontaneously spring out of the heads of a few crazy zealots,

"The energy for this radicalism is channeled from the explosive discontent felt throughout the Islamic world at the dislocations of globalization, persistent poverty and what is felt as the intrusion of American culture into traditional societies."

Although the terrorism which was rained down upon us this week is completely unacceptable (and has no moral justification whatever) it nonetheless has decades-old root causes that we (and other nations in the developed world) must eventually address with diligent diplomacy, structures of greater social and economic justice, and (eventually) a whole new way of doing business in the world that is more just, respectful and fair to all.

Surely you all understand that we cannot bomb or kill our way out of this or any other of our world's most persistent problems and conflicts.

Third, (and this is very important for us, especially in this region where we share life with so many Americans of Arabic descent) there is the danger that some American citizens (out of their irrational and uncontrolled anger) will commit immoral and unjust acts of violence, prejudice and hatred against innocent Arabic people -- both here and abroad. The newspapers have already reported some isolated but disturbing incidences of such misdirected hate. Please...please...wherever you go...whomever you speak with...as a religious person, express your ABSOLUTE REFUSAL to stereotype any human being, and give voice to your COMPLETE COMMITMENT to protect the civil rights and inherent worth and dignity of all citizens - no matter where they come from in the world, no matter what their spoken tongue or chosen faith.

Yes, as a people, we are grieving, and we are fearful, and we are very angry.

But these primordial emotions are no excuse for abrogating our highest American principles nor our humanity. I pray that as a people we will never forget that there are always, always, ALWAYS powerful, honorable, and less-violent options open to us...peaceful options which -- in the long run - may prove to be far better than knee-jerk, indiscriminate violence for both our nation and the world.

Over the coming days, there will be many voices being raised in America about what we must do, and when we must do it. There will be strident voices (and there will be measured ones). There will be irrational voices (and there

First Sunday

will be reasoned ones). There will be hateful voices (and there will be compassionate ones). I pray that each and every one of you, as an American, will lift your voices on behalf of the best that is in your heart and live the finest from your faith tradition. I pray that you will lift your voices on behalf of the principles of our Unitarian Universalist faith, and in defense of those parallel values which lie at the true and beautiful heart of the American dream.

Though in so many ways (right now) we all feel ineffectual and uncertain, each of us can and must speak and act to make a positive, principled difference in our world. Each of us, as helpless as we are sometimes feeling, can and must choose to embody in our living what is true and loving, and humane and right.

It is on all our faces this morning. We are all profoundly shaken. No one (not even those who are speaking the loudest and angriest) truly knows what to do, nor why and how to do it. No one (not even those who pretend to know everything) can take away the uncertainty and angst of this painful American moment. Let us, then, keep our emotional and moral bearings. Let us remain wise, and loving, and resolute people of faith. Let us gently but-insistently speak and live the principles and values that animate our hearts. Let us refuse to lose our nobility and compassion just because great wrong has been done against us.

Donald Robert Elton & Aura Agudo Elton

Yes, I hate what has happened. No, the world is not as simple or safe a place as it was early last Tuesday morning. And surely incredibly perilous and uncertain days lie ahead...all of us will be regularly troubled and tested. I leave you, then, simply with this prayer, my dear friends, to hold you safe until we gather here again in faith, hope and love:

Be of good courage...

Refuse all negation...

Stand up for that which is best and brightest in your heart...

Believe in yourself, and the role you have to play in the positive unfolding of our world...
Offer yourself boldly in the days ahead -- in love...in compassion...in peacefulness...in justice and in hope...

Know that you are not alone, and there is much good you can do with others of good will...
And pray with me now - pray with all your heart -- that our human family (every precious part of it) will find the way to a more just and peaceful future for all...

I love you...be safe...be strong...and never, ever forget what you believe, and how you must live.
Amen.

First Sunday

Rev. George Antonakos

Central Presbyterian Church
Baltimore, Maryland

Sunday, September 16, 2001

When I think back to that week, we were all reeling in the wake of the tragedy and it became immediately clear that everything being planned would have to be put on hold. I asked the Lord to show me a passage that might be related to the emotions of the moment and felt as though he did. That was the goal, to be a voice of comfort for any who would be present with a special awareness that many might be in attendance that were not normally in church.

I only recall one response to the sermon this far beyond the event. The person shared that he felt that the message was what was needed and that God had led me in it. I don't recall any specific connections to the actual crisis; we were like hundreds of thousands of other congregations in being challenged to pray for those who were most affected.

I am still very much saddened every time I see a movie with the Twin Towers in the NYC skyline. It feels like the national wound will not be healed until we see the new Freedom Tower dedicated and then maybe it will take longer. I recall the day it happened, saying what I think many baby boomers must have said – "Now I know how my parents and many others felt about Pearl Harbor."

As strongly as I did feel about this tragic event I was not in favor of the Iraq War. I felt almost as sad the day it was reported that we were striking Baghdad as I did 9-11. I knew that many innocents were going to die and thought we still needed to assess what our response should be.

And of course that brings us to present day feelings about radical Islamists. We still must be vigilant not hateful in return. In the past year or so I've read Greg Mortensen's <u>Three Cups of Tea</u> *and* <u>Stones into Schools</u>. *And I am grateful that those books have informed our military leaders. How much we need to try and understand, pray for and love our enemies to demonstrate the life and heart of our Lord.*

God, Don't You Care?

Theme: Only Jesus can calm the storms (insecurity) of life.

Today all of us gather here with a vast mixture of emotions and not just with emotions but also by reactions to the incredible, indescribable events of this past week. We have all experienced, I believe, a collective trauma and some of us are still in a state of shock and disbelief. Others are keeping the pain at arm's length and still others are filled with sadness, or rage, or both. In prayer this week I cried out to God, tears running down my cheeks, "I hate them, I hate them. I hate them." And then in other times I

First Sunday

struggled, completely by faith, to pray for forgiveness because my heart wasn't in it. It's been hard to concentrate, our hearts are filled with pain, our minds are tired, and people tell me that they can't do much work. Wednesday morning I awoke hoping that it was all a bad dream. It was almost like someone in my immediate family had died. I've felt like that all through the week, and no matter how many times I saw again and again the collisions and the collapse of the Twin Towers, there was still a part of me that could not believe it. Like you, every time, I listen to a story of someone's loss or see the pained expression on the face of a loved one losing hope, my heart breaks. Sadness, rage, and fear intermingle. And then during the week I said, "Lord what should I say on Sunday?" Seeking inspiration, I looked at my desk calendar at home. It was pages off of the right date. So I flipped it to September 11 to see what scripture it quoted for the day. The quote was Zephaniah 1:15. I had forgotten that Zephaniah was even part of the Bible, but this is what it said. "That day will be a day of wrath, a day of distress and anguish. A day of ruin and devastation, a day of darkness and gloom, a day of clouds and thick darkness." There couldn't be a better image of the day God comes to judge the earth, than this past week, especially as seen in Dr. Mark Heath's video that was taken only blocks away as one of the towers came down in clouds of smoke and showers of concrete. Then, for 30 seconds on the video you couldn't see anything even though it was a bright day. I said, "Lord is this what I am supposed to preach?" I'll feel like one of those guys on the street corner that everybody mocks, if I hold up a sign and say, "Repent, the end of the world is near." Lord, how about another text? A text that teaches what it might feel like for people who thought they were about to live their last day. People who thought that their world was caving in and their end was near. So, listen now to Mark, Chapter 4:35-41 from the gospel of our Lord Jesus.

"That day when evening came he said to his disciples, 'Let us go over to the other side.' Leaving the crowd behind they took him along just as he was in the boat. There were also other boats with him. A furious squall came up and the waves broke over the boat, so that it was nearly swamped. Jesus was in the stern sleeping on a cushion. The disciples woke him and said to him, 'Teacher, don't you care if we drown?' He got up, rebuked the wind and said to the waves, 'Quiet, be still.' Then the wind died down and it was completely calm. He said to his disciples, 'Why are you so afraid? Do you still have no faith?' They were terrified and asked each other, 'Who is this?

Even the wind and the waves obey him.

John Wesley was making a transatlantic voyage when his ship encountered a fierce storm. He and others clung to their bunks and hid their heads. Also on that ship was a group of Moravian Brethren Christians. At the appointed time, just as they did every day, they calmly gathered to hold their daily worship service and sing praises to God,

First Sunday

much as we have done this morning. John Wesley, the founder of the Methodist Church, was impressed. From that moment on he prayed that God would give him the ability to likewise ride out life's storms with the same confidence he saw demonstrated that day. Friends, on September 11, America and the world, was hit by a terroristic wave that has us reeling in a storm of evil. And this familiar text teaches us some important truths that will help us be like the Moravians who were on John Wesley's ship. This is not a profound sermon. I only have three reflections on this text. And here's the first.

Even though Jesus was smack dab in the middle of that boat, with his disciples, they were not spared the storm. The clouds and wind didn't say, "Oh, there's Jesus, we better go around. And there are his disciples, faithfully serving him. We'd better side skirt them, too." In fact, the clouds and wind hit so hard that professional fisherman thought they were going to die. And when that happens you know it's got to be a bad storm. Have you ever seen that show on the Discovery Channel, "Savage Seas?" If you have, you are aware of the terror of a bad storm. In this world, we are not spared the storms of trouble and pain. But as we will soon see, the Lord in our midst will help us through the storm and we can outlast it. I want to say something about the stormy sea from a theological angle. In many Near Eastern mythologies and in Jewish apocalyptic literature, which is literature that describes the end days and judgment, the sea is specifically identified as a realm of evil. In Revelation 13:1, John describes images of the dragon and the beast, images of evil that indicate that the dragon is standing by the shore of the sea and then the passage says that the beast will come up out of the sea. Then in Chapter 21, John says, "Then I saw a new heaven and a new earth, for the first heaven and the first earth had passed away, and there was no longer any sea." The sea is spoken of as an arena of conflict between God and Satan.

You know if you were to look back at the earlier part of Mark, we are in Chapter 4, if you were to look from Mark, Chapter 1 to where we are, you would see seven or eight references of Jesus encountering Satan or demons. And in the text right after the storm on the sea, is Jesus casting the demons into the herd of swine and they rush into the sea. Mark is busy trying to tell us something. That Jesus confronts, and conquers, and masters the evil that we encounter in this world.

Back in Mark 1:24, there is an evil spirit of a demon possessed man who cries out, "What do you want with us Jesus of Nazareth?" Have you come to destroy us? I know who you are, you're the Holy one of God." He said, "Be quiet." And the demon came out. And amazed the people said, "What is this, a new teaching?" You see we are not spared from storms. Storms are those times that we believe that we are in a situation that even God can't handle. When we feel totally vulnerable and hopeless, we have hit a storm.

First Sunday

One of the survivors who was on the 71st floor of the second tower was interviewed and he said, "If I had been in the first tower, I would not be here today." Those 18 minutes allowed me to escape and he said, "You know you realize how fragile life is when it's measured in minutes." It's not a shame to be afraid in the storm. And being hit by a storm doesn't mean we have done something wrong, it means that there is great evil in this world, but it's not an uncontrollable evil.

The second thing I would like to say about this text is that the disciples, even in the midst of their desperation, finally looked in the right direction. My guess is that at first they were looking at each other. They were probably saying, "C'mon John grab that sail harder." "Andrew, steer, row." Some of you may come here today and say, "Pastor, tell us, preach harder, give us answers." I am just a bailing disciple, just like you. And I say, "What are you looking at me for?" Look at him! He's the only one who can help at this time. The problem for many people is they have never hit a big enough storm. They have never come to the end of their limits or themselves. Have you found yourself praying more in the last five days? Why? Because we realize how dependent we are on God. And we are desperately aware of our limits. That's what storms are. They bring us up short of our limits.

You know one of the great dangers that we face today is to

rely on our military might. Please do not misunderstand what I am saying. I want us to bring someone to justice as much as anyone, but if we are not looking to Jesus, we are not looking in the right direction. The scripture says, the arm of the flesh will fail. It is vain to trust in princes. Our trust is in the Lord who strengthens us. But some may be saying what the disciples are saying, which is, "Don't you care if we drown?" That's what they said. The disciples said, "Don't you care, Lord, that we are drowning?" "God, don't you care? How can I trust you? It seems like you're sleeping. Don't you care?" Yes, he cares. That's why he was in the boat with those twelve human beings. God became a human being and he cares so much that he took on evil full force on the cross. So that he might bring you and me back to Him, so that he might confront the evil that lives in each one of our hearts and forgive us and make us right with Him.

I can think of at least three reasons why they didn't need to be fearful in the trouble. First, they had Jesus' promise. He said, "Let's go over to the other side." They had his promise that they were going to go to the other side. Secondly, they had his presence. He was right there in the boat with them. And thirdly, they had seen his power. For weeks on end he had been doing all kinds of things to demonstrate his power over evil and he was completely at peace sleeping in the midst of the storm. And we have these same things available to us, these same indicators. The great danger is not the storm, it's unbelief.

First Sunday

And that brings us to our third point. That the disciples needed to understand their main problem was internal, not external. Our greatest problems are always those within us, not those around us. Jesus did calm the storm. He did take care of their fears. He did stand up and look at the wind and waves and said, "Quiet, be still." But he didn't take care just of their fear, and just of their felt needs, he went deeper to look at their unfelt needs and he said, "Why are you so afraid? Do you still have no faith?" And they said, "Who is this?" They were terrified, they said, "Who is this that even wind and the waves obey him?" I know that 99% of us here today probably have deep faith in Jesus. I would say that if you don't have deep faith in Jesus, if you don't trust him alone in times like this, turn to him. He is the only one that can help us. But I want to ask you--do you really know whom you say you believe in? Do you really know who is traveling with us? He said, "All authority in heaven and earth has been given to me. Not some, not most--all authority in heaven and earth has been given to me." Turn all that you know of yourself to all that you know of him. And he will calm your heart through this storm as well.

Many of us know the story of Horatio Spafford. Horatio Spafford penned the hymn we are about to sing. For those of you who don't know, Horatio Spafford was waiting on his wife and children to cross the Atlantic. And midway across, a storm capsized their ship and his family was lost.

On his return voyage, he asked the captain to stop somewhere in the area where he believed his family's ship capsized. And as Spafford looked over the side of his ship he penned these words,

"It is well with my soul. When peace like a river attendth my way, when sorrows like sea billows roll. Whatever my lot, thou hast taught me to say. It is well, it is well with my soul."

The Psalmist, King David, knew this peace as well and he said what the choir often sings. But I want to read it to you again to close out this sermon and to remind you that God alone is our hope. "I will lie down and sleep in peace, for you alone, Oh Lord, make me dwell in safety."

With understanding, let us now stand and sing our prayers by singing, "It is well with my soul."

First Sunday

Pastor Daniel B. Barker
Cortland Trinity Baptist Church
Cortland, OH

September 15, 2001

It has been nine years since 9-11. Many of the things associated with that day have faded but some of the feelings and responses of my own heart will always remain.

The day of the 9-11 attacks the pastors in Cortland, Ohio called a meeting to discuss all that had happened and how we could best respond. We decided to conduct a Community Prayer Service and hold it at the local High School football stadium the next day, September 12. Various pastors would share personal thoughts and lead in prayers for our nation. I was asked to bring a message from God's word.

That night, as I thought about what to share at this community event, I could not deny my own feelings of anger at what had been done to my nation. I could not get the images of planes flying into the twin towers, people jumping to their deaths and sky scrapers crumbling to the ground out of my mind. I knew most Americans shared my anger. It became clear the Lord wanted me to make America's anger the focus of my message. He brought Ephesians 4:26 to my mind; "Be angry, and do not sin, do not let the sun go down on your wrath." As I developed the sermon around this theme the Lord helped me put my own anger in perspective and I knew He would do the same for others. I asked Him to meet with us the next day knowing He would be faithful to help us in our time of need.

Several hundred people came to the Community Prayer Service. They sat in the bleachers waiting to hear something to help them cope with the shocking events of the previous day. God indeed was faithful. He gave us some very practical ways to deal with our anger and "overcome evil with good."

Shortly after this the Lord directed us to produce a patriotic program called, "America You're Beautiful." It was a multimedia tribute to our Christian heritage and a call to repentance and prayer. Over the next three years the Lord opened doors for us to share this message of hope in many places.

God's faithfulness to our nation in the wake of 9-11 reminds me of His awesome ability to bring good out of tragedy. Four years ago God dropped into the hearts of some fifteen pastors to meet on a weekly basis to pray for revival and the Trumbull County Prayer Movement was birthed. In spite of our nation's crises we are renewed with hope concerning all the good God wants to bring to us today if we will turn to Him with all our hearts.

First Sunday

America's Response to Terrorism's Attack

The greatest terrorist attack in the history of our nation unfolded before our very eyes on Tuesday, September 11, 2001. The unthinkable became reality. The World Trade Center towers, standing 100 stories high above the New York City skyline, crumbled to the ground one hour after being hit by two commercial airliners flown by terrorist hijackers. Almost simultaneously a crashed terrorist driven plane also hit the Pentagon. Some are calling it, "America's Second Day of Infamy." These acts of terrorism have changed our world forever. Life in America will never be the same. More than a crime, these were acts of war! President Bush called it, "The evil acts of a faceless coward." Undoubtedly, the death toll from these terrorist attacks will produce the greatest number of casualties the United States has ever experienced in any other military encounter, outnumbering Pearl Harbor and D-day. Our nation is gripped with fear, confusion and anger.

WHAT WILL BE OUR RESPONSE TO THESE SENSELESS ACTS?

A gentleman from our church approached me following a prayer service we conducted last night, bothered by the fact that he was feeling so much anger. Knowing the scripture tells us to forgive, he felt his anger was inappropriate. An investigation of scripture shows us that

God gives us permission to be angry at a time like this.

"Be angry, and do not sin, do not let the sun go down on your wrath." Ephesians 4:26

"Be angry…" Anger is a God given emotion. It has a good purpose. There is a good reason why God gave us the ability to experience anger. Anger is "God's warning signal" that something wrong, something inappropriate is happening…preparing us to make an appropriate response. All of us will agree that yesterday's attack on civilians with the intent of destroying many innocent lives is horrifically wrong! President Bush referred to America's "quiet and unyielding anger," during his speech to the nation last evening.

And so, being angry at a time like this is normal, even good. The question is not, "Should we be angry?" but rather, "What do we do with our anger?" What is an appropriate response?

"…do not sin…" What we do with our anger is our responsibility. God tells us to be angry but not to sin in our anger. He wants us to take our anger and do something constructive with it. Abraham Lincoln saw the injustice done to black slaves when he was a teenager and in his anger he said, "Someday I will do something about this!" His anger motivated him to do something good when he saw the evil around him.

First Sunday

Ways we can sin in our anger:

1. We can deny our anger, and stuff it, or ignore it. "I'm a Christian, I shouldn't be feeling anger!" This doesn't change the fact that legitimate anger is still there and that anger will manifest itself in other ways in our lives…ways that are unhealthy.

2. We can allow our anger to turn into hate. When anger is not given a healthy outlet, it will turn into resentment and bitterness…even hatred. Hating the people who did this will do more harm to us than it will to them. Now is not the time for racial prejudice.

3. We can become aggressive, and take matters into our own hands. Lashing out at all Arabic people, wishing to inflict harm on others or carrying out our own "hate missions," and reduce ourselves to the level of those who have sinned against us.

Ways we can constructively use our anger.

4. We can desire justice. I believe it is normal and healthy for us to have a sense of justice that cries out for consequences for evil acts. This is certainly not a time for indifference or ambivalence! There cries out from the soul of America a call for justice to be served. A desire for justice is a desire for the safety of our children, our

families, and our society. I believe America expects our government to respond to this aggression; I believe America needs to see our government respond! But instead of taking matters into our own hands let us allow those in authority to take the appropriate actions to bring those responsible to justice. God has ordained governmental authority to deal with evil, as Paul clearly stated in Romans 12.

5. We can use our energy and resources for good. Firefighters from Seattle and Arizona have gone to NY to help with rescue efforts. We can call the Red Cross and give blood. We can send financial relief to hurting and people devastated by loss and grief. We can support our President and our military personnel. We can cooperate with what will surely be, more stringent measures of security throughout our nation in the days ahead. Take the energy of anger and do good!

6. We can pray! We can take the energy of anger and direct it toward God! The presence of sin, evil and injustice in the world should drive us to God! In Psalm 50:15 God says, "Call upon Me in the day of trouble; I will deliver you, and you shall glorify Me." The Psalms are full of petitions by David and others, calling out to God for justice and deliverance from evil enemies. When we see how hopeless we truly are against evil we seek the God of goodness and holiness to come to our aid. Not all of our anger is for the enemies of our nation. Our anger also reminds us of the sin

First Sunday

and evil in our own hearts and compels us to confess our sins. There are some serious questions that America needs to answer in the face of these attacks.

~ Have we as a nation placed our confidence in our economy instead of God?

~ Have we bowed before the idol of materialism and wealth?

~ In our prosperity, have we forgotten God?

~ Are these attacks on our country a "wake up call" for America?

God is our very present help in the time of trouble. He is our rock. He is our defense. He is our God and we will trust in Him.

The World Trade Center towers were home to some of the great financial institutions of America. They stood as a representation of our economy and our faith in money. In the space of a few minutes of time, they came crashing down. But Proverbs 18:10 reminds us of a tower that is unshakable and beyond the reach of all evil that might attempt to bring it down. Hear of this great tower and take heart all you citizens of Cortland, Ohio and Trumbull County.

"The name of the LORD is a strong tower; the righteous run to it and are safe!" (Proverbs 18:10) Indeed, God has provided a "safe harbor" for all of us in the cross of His Son, Jesus Christ. Christ is the Great Shepherd who will protect His sheep. President Bush quoted Psalm 23 in his message to the nation saying, "Though I walk through the valley of the shadow of death, I will fear no evil…for You are with me." As long as our words agree with the Psalmist's words in Psalm 56:3-4, we will be alright.

"Whenever I am afraid, I will trust in You. In God I have put my trust, I will not fear! What can flesh do to me?"

Martin Luther's words, which he penned many years ago are so appropriate now.

A mighty fortress is our God, a bulwark never failing. Our Helper He amid the flood, of mortal ills prevailing. For still our ancient foe, doth seek to work us woe, His craft and power are great and armed with cruel hate, On earth is not his equal.

Did we in our own strength confide, our striving would be losing; Were not the right man on our side, the man of God's own choosing. Dost ask who that may be? Christ Jesus it is He, Lord Sabbath His name, From age to age the same, and He must win the battle.

And tho this world with devils filled, should threaten to

First Sunday

undo us, We will not fear for God hath willed, His truth to triumph through us. The prince of darkness grim, we tremble not for him; His rage we can endure; for lo his doom is sure, One little word shall fell him.

That word above all earthly powers, no thanks to them abideth. The Spirit and the gifts are ours, thru Him who with us sideth. Let goods and kindred go, this mortal life also, the body they may kill; God's truth abideth still. His kingdom is forever.

Martin Luther "A Mighty Fortress is Our God."

Donald Robert Elton & Aura Agudo Elton

Rev. M. Craig Barnes

The National Presbyterian Church
Washington, DC

September 16, 2001

Response to Crisis: Under Attack; Under God

Psalms 46:1-7
On Monday I planned to preach about something else today. On Tuesday I knew that for the first time in twenty years, I would have to change the sermon. A lot of things changed on Tuesday ... probably more than we know. Whether or not the nation changes for the better in the days ahead will depend on our ability to see ourselves not only as a nation under attack but also under God.

Lord God, we gather this morning in churches all over the world, all of us more open than ever before to a holy word from You. Do now what only your Spirit can do. Speak into our souls. Amen.

As a pastor who has spent a lot of time in the emergency rooms of life, I am accustomed to the profoundly sad, numb feelings that arise from the soul in a crisis. All week it felt like the whole nation was in an emergency room. There is only one thing that we have been thinking about. Everything else, all other business, seems unimportant and even profane.

First Sunday

Like an anxious family stuck in the waiting room, we have had an insatiable thirst for news about what happened. "Have you heard?" we asked. "How did it happen? How bad is it?" Then, like a family that learns things are very bad, we know that we will never be the same again. We will recover, but the nation will never be the same again.

Sooner or later every individual ends up in the emergency room. Something happens that you were not planning on, something that permanently alters the plans you had. Maybe a loved one dies, a deadly disease is discovered, or a cherished relationship unravels. When that happens, you realize you will not leave the emergency room the same person you were when you entered. That is exactly where our nation is today. Wounded with a broken heart and certain only that things have changed.

As we leave the emergency room and make decisions about how we get on with life, let us remember that the nation is strong. It is strong enough to survive this atrocity. Actually, it is strong enough to do more than survive. It can become a different, better nation than we were on Monday. But that all depends on the choices we make in the days ahead.

The French Philosopher Paul Ricoeur has written about the creative possibility of "limit experiences." A limit experience is an experience that is beyond the limits of normal life. It's the one you spent most of life avoiding, dreading, defending yourself against, like death and separation. Beyond the limits of those things, we think there's nothing but emptiness, loss and anomie. But as Dr. Ricoeur reminds us, there is more. There is also God whose creative love knows no limits.

Watching enormous skyscrapers crumble into dust is beyond the limits of comprehension. It doesn't matter how many times we watch the video, it's still beyond comprehension. As is seeing a gaping wound in the side of the Pentagon. And imagining how men can be so evil as to crash full airplanes into these buildings. And understanding how thousands could so easily die on our own well-protected soil. It's all beyond our limits.

Be clear. None of that was the will of God. It was not a judgment against us, retribution for our sins, or God teaching us a lesson. Rather the will of God is always that evil be redeemed and not given the last word. That is why God can always be found at work beyond the limits of evil's destructive powers, waiting to bring us back to new life.

The greatest catastrophe of history happened not on Tuesday, but two thousand years ago when we crucified the Son of God. That was the ultimate experience beyond humanity's limit. But it was then that history was given the possibility of resurrection. When Jesus Christ defeated

First Sunday

death, He did so that we may experience something beyond our limits -- to rise with Him into a new life. After every cross, the resurrection remains a possibility. The stone that covers the tomb is rolled back, but it is up to us to emerge as a new nation. It all depends on the choices we make.

If our choices arise out of a new vision of service and justice, if we now commit ourselves to something greater than collecting more and more personal wealth, and if we unite around our leaders and stop whining about how small a piece of the American pie they are giving us, then we'll emerge from this tragedy as a nation ready to fulfill its calling in the earth. But if our future choices arise out of fear, we might as well stay in the tomb.

Near the end of the week, I took a break from reading newspapers to look again at Tom Brokaw's popular book, The Greatest Generation. As I reviewed all of those wonderful stories of the World War II generation, I was struck by the ordinariness of the lives he was describing. No one in that war was born a hero. But as they were pushed beyond the limits they found something heroic in their souls they did not know was there. It wasn't that the hard times made the hero. Hard times are just hard. Heroes are ordinary people who refuse to be governed by fear when times are hard.

Is this not also what inspired us this week as we heard about ordinary men and women rising above their fear to overtake the hijackers, firemen sacrificing their lives in the line of duty and rescue workers tirelessly digging through the rubble searching for survivors while buildings fell down around them? When you heard those stories, you couldn't help but ask yourself, "What about me? Could I do that?" It all depends on how you handle fear.

You don't have to wait until you're in a hijacked plane to find out if you can rise above fear. That was their moment. This is ours -- the moment that follows the crises. The moment we leave the emergency room to form a new spirit in this nation. If we are afraid, we will spend all our energy arguing over blame. We will waste this moment by retreating into a national fortress, and we will allow the terrorists to win by terrorizing us. But if we refuse to be afraid, we will unite this great country into a new creation that looks a lot more like the new kingdom Jesus talked about. The soul of the nation can go either way, depending on how we respond to this moment.

This is not the first great hour of decision our nation has faced about its soul, and we are not the first nation to face it. But historically each generation receives only one opportunity. This is ours, and we dare not miss it.

The Bible reminds us that Jerusalem faced such an hour whenever it was attacked and threatened. Generation after

First Sunday

generation struggled to rise above their fear and act like a holy, just people. Some generations succeeded. Some did not. This is what the Psalmist was addressing when he wrote, "God is our refuge and strength, a very present help in trouble. Therefore we will not fear, though the earth should change ...." Well, the earth has changed. For us, it changed last Tuesday. Whether or not the earth changes for good depends on where we go for refuge and strength.

If we believe as the Psalmist says, "God is in the midst of the city; it shall not be moved," then we shall not be moved. "Though the earth change, though the mountains shake in the heart of the sea, though its waters roar and foam," we shall not be moved! Not because we are so strong or invincible, but because we take refuge in the God who is in our midst. When we can see that God is with us, then we know that even when we are pushed beyond the limits, God will be waiting there to lead us into a new risen life together.

"God is in the midst of the city." He is not sitting indifferently above and beyond the horrific destruction we witnessed this week. Perhaps you saw the television interview of the distressed woman who lamented, "Where was God when the planes crashed into those buildings?" I can answer that: in the midst of the city. He was in the offices that collapsed down upon each other as the towers crumbled. He was under the rubble where the dead and wounded lay buried. He was in the planes filled with terrified passengers that called to warn us of what was happening or to say goodbye to their families. God was in the midst of all that pathos. As the cross of Jesus Christ proclaims, God can always be found in the places of suffering. He is there not simply to comfort, but to lead us to resurrected life.

At the end of the fourth century when the city of Rome was being attacked by barbaric tribes from the North, St. Augustine was called upon to provide a theological interpretation of those days. In response he wrote a classic philosophy of history called The City of God. Augustine claimed that from the beginning there have always been only two cities in history: the city of self-love and the city of God's love. One of these cities may be more visible, but they exist in the same place at the same time, and you have to choose to which city you really belong. Since the city of self-love is motivated by greed, it always eventually decays from the inside out. Every empire, every city of earth that prides itself on itself has not survived. But the city of God will always persevere, like the love of God in our midst.

What our society is deciding in the weeks and months ahead is which city we will be. Maybe for too long we have flirted with self-love. Maybe we have deluded ourselves thinking that we could each live for ourselves, or that the nation existed only to serve our individual needs. If this country is to survive, we will have to start looking like the other city. We have to start living for a holy purpose greater than ourselves and demonstrating the love of God to each other.

I can tell you we are off to a good start. Our leaders are weighing carefully the options for how we must proceed. Volunteers have come out of the woodwork, and people are waiting five hours to donate blood. Flags are everywhere, as if we have discovered we belong to a nation. Now it falls to the houses of worship to teach people how to pray again and live out of God's word. And it falls to each of you to make a critical decision about the sacred purposes of your life. A nation is nothing more than the collective souls of its people, and this nation is counting on you to know how to live all your life under God.

I am not only calling you to nationalism or patriotism. I'm calling you to something even greater. I'm echoing the Bible's call to come out from the tombs, embrace the gift of life and follow Jesus as He leads us into a future filled with hope.

O God, when we face an evil day that pushes us way beyond the limits of our experience, may we find refuge in your perfect love that casts out all fear, making room for heroes.
Amen.

Rev. David M. Bryce

The First Church in Belmont, UU
Belmont, Massachusetts

Saturday, September 15, 2001

I "prepared" for the sermon by watching television for days; like most people I was initially shocked and numbed. I also spent hours asking myself what I could possibly say about this horrendous and shattering occurrence.

Initially I hoped to put the events into some perspective for myself. I have described my sermons as conversations that I have with myself which others are listening in on; and this sermon was no exception to that. I was seeking a way that I could comprehend, understand and then draw some meaning out of the actions of that day and its aftermath for myself with the hope that I would also receive some comfort from this.

However, I also understood the weighty responsibility that I had as a minister. I knew that people would be coming to services that Sunday seeking the very comprehension, understanding, meaning and comfort that I was seeking for myself and did not yet have. I knew that I had to find some way to express these and to point towards hope.

First Sunday

I also wanted one more thing; I wanted to avoid or eliminate the anger and desire for vengeance that I knew was alive in me and certainly was alive in others. I wanted to invoke and speak to the higher self in each of us, the self that could claim and feel compassion for all of the dead, including the attackers. Not easy to feel, not easy to call for, not easy to have others hear.

The congregation to which I preached this sermon (The First Unitarian Society of Westchester in Hastings-On-Hudson, NY), is in the suburbs of New York City; it is just a twenty minute train ride to Grand Central. This attack was very much in our "back yard." Though none of the congregants were killed or injured, a large percentage of the congregation worked in New York, some in the downtown financial district where the World Trade Center was located. One of them walked all the way from downtown up to the northern tip of Manhattan and across into the Bronx. One of them owned a decommissioned fire boat; since public transportation was shut down following the attacks he used his boat to ferry people from the New York to the New Jersey side of the Hudson River so they could get home.

Several in the congregation knew people who had died in the attacks. I knew two people (non-congregants) whose siblings had died.

I do not know how the congregation was influenced by the sermon; I hope the result was hope and comfort.

I appreciate more than ever the soul searching that Americans did following the attacks. Many of us were reminded that money and the possession of things are not the purpose in life; that love, compassion and relationships matter much more.

In the days following the attacks I was fearful that the understandable anger of Americans would lead to a self-righteous anger which would result in striking out at others. And, indeed, I am deeply saddened that instead of being moved to build a world of peace and justice the government of the United States used September 11 as the excuse for an irrational invasion of Iraq.

I also regret that the same anger seems to have seeped into our body politic, intensifying the divisions that already existed between Americans. We are a better people than our behavior would indicate. I hope that the remembrances of 9-11 will call us to our better selves.

Living In A Time Of Darkness

In a few days summer slips away and autumn begins, reminding us of the ongoing cycle of seasons, of the ongoing cycle of life. Autumn is the season when the days grow noticeably shorter, the leaves fall, harvests are

First Sunday

brought in; it is the time then the world seems to die and fade into winter; but it is also the time when the world is reborn.

This past week, things happened which shook most of us. Things happened which are still difficult even to believe. I have seen the videos over and over again, and still part of me does not believe that these events have actually taken place.

If you have come here expecting that you will hear from me words that will make sense of these acts, know that I find them unfathomable; if you have come here to find words of faith, know that my faith is shaken; if you have come here to find words of hope, know that my hope is fragile.

We have been reminded this week, in ways that we do not wish to be, that life itself is a fragile thing at best, that our sense of what is can be swept away in one moment. We are faced with the stark truth that anything we take for granted - anything - can be gone in an instant; and with that truth right before us we can lose our sense of security.

Still there is hope, and we must keep alive the spirit of hope for ourselves, for any who may still be alive under that building, for their families, and for those still digging in the rubble. But must also face the reality that MOST of those people are gone; some never to be found.

And we must face the reality that something fundamental is gone from our lives: assumptions of security and safety; assumptions about life; and for some of us, assumptions about the goodness of humanity and the universe.

I have felt many emotions over the past few days: first came surprise and confusion. Then there was a growing sense of shock; shock and horror that grew with each new detail. With that was a sense of unreality; this was too immense to grasp. Then came incredible sadness. In some moments I found myself with tears streaming down my face; in the next moment I might feel nothing, just numbness.

Today, one of my emotions is anger, deep anger; even a desire for vengeance. It is not my ONLY emotion, but it is there.

I have also been deeply touched by outpouring of grief and support from people around the world. There was a moment of silence that was observed from London to Moscow. People paused for silence even in Iran. The Cold Stream Guard playing our national anthem, and hearing it sung at the beginning of the worship service in St Paul's Cathedral; these were heartfelt acts. (I was not unaware of the Ironic fact that our anthem was written to commemorate events that took place during a battle between American forces and British troops; and here now

First Sunday

were British troops playing our anthem.)

Donald Robert Elton & Aura Agudo Elton

I have found myself humming the national anthem, and on Tuesday evening I found myself looking for the lapel flag pin that I used to have.

I understand this welling of patriotism in myself and in others. But I must tell you that I am also wary when the flag is waved too loudly and boldly, because I know where that can lead. So today, I have another emotion besides anger and patriotism, and that is fear; fear for what is to come, both at home and abroad.

And I fear that very fear, and the anger I feel within me and in this nation.

I pray that there will be no ongoing cycle of rage and violence.

I know that when there is anger there is also a search for someone to blame.

I have heard the words of blame already: who would design a building that was so tall that firefighters could not reach the upper stories of it? Who told people in Tower Two to go back to their desks? Who allowed these hijackers to get on the planes with knives?

How we respond to these events can unite us or can damage our nation, our society.

First Sunday

You may have read the Washington Post report in which Jerry Falwell and Pat Robertson blame pagans, feminists, abortionists, gays and lesbians, the American Civil Liberties union and People For the American Way for these tragedies; they said that it was removing God from our schools and from public life that caused this. That is to say that we here are to blame; almost everyone in this room is on that list. We as a nation, we as a society, cannot afford that kind of response, because it can tear us apart.

Some Americans have the desire for revenge and have wrongly turned their anger on people who they know or who appear to them to be Muslim, Arab or from other Middle Eastern nations. This is a betrayal of genuine patriotism and of our common humanity. As Americans, as believers in human rights, as people of Faith, as people who believe in the inherent worth and dignity of every person, as people who oppose bigotry of all kinds, it is our responsibility to accept and affirm, to support and, where necessary, to protect those of our brothers and sisters who are Muslim or of Middle Eastern heritage.

I hope that I can be big enough, good enough, spiritual enough, to have compassion for all people.

I hope I can be big enough, good enough, spiritual enough to have compassion for Jerry Falwell and Pat Robertson. They are as confused as we are, and are searching to make sense and reason of this just as we are.

And I hope I am big enough, good enough, spiritual enough to have compassion even for those who allow their anger to lead them into inappropriate behavior against their brothers and sisters who are Muslim.

I hope that I have understanding for the anger of those who react in such ways, but we cannot allow people's justifiable anger to be vented at the innocent. And no one is guilty just because of their nationality, their racial or ethnic group, or their religious affiliation. We must reject any concept of group guilt, any stereotyping, within ourselves, within other people and in our nation.

We, all of us, we as individuals, we as a people, we as a nation, must learn to allow ourselves to be angry; but not to act on that anger in ways which themselves are unjust, which themselves are outrages. We must fight within ourselves the desire to find a scapegoat.

That applies to we as a nation as well.

Our national anger and outrage is justified.

Now, how do we respond?

People have done a terrible thing to us and we have a desire to punish them for it.

First Sunday

The mark of our character as individuals and as a nation is not whether bad things happen to us, but how we respond to them.

Will we now, as a nation, show wisdom? Will we take actions that isolate those individuals who are dangerous and protect and build the security of all of the people of the world?

Or will we take actions which themselves instill the same pain and suffering on others that we now feel so that someday some people in some room somewhere in this world are saying to themselves: those criminal Americans have done such a terrible thing to us that they deserve to be punished.

As we ought to have compassion for those who are so outraged at this that they lash out at their neighbors, so we must have compassion for our own anger and ourselves. But in either case, while affirming the justified feelings, we must not allow those feelings to be vented at innocent people or to result in wrong actions.

Let us remember to target our emotions it at those who carried out these acts and died doing so.

I believe, also, that there is one more group of people for whom we must feel compassion; and this is difficult.

Donald Robert Elton & Aura Agudo Elton

Our Universalist heritage challenges us to love ALL people, to love EVERY person, to see every individual as a child of God or of the Universe, as a brother or a sister.

We must recognize the rage that so twisted the minds and souls of the perpetrators of these acts that they sacrificed their own lives and the lives of thousands of innocent people to their cause. What they did was monstrous. No decent or rational person can condone their actions

I must say as an aside here that as a child of the sixties, as an anti-Vietnam War activist, I remember May 5, 1970, when I heard about the killings at Kent State. I was so enraged that I came to believe that nonviolence was not the answer, that the American government was so evil that it was beyond the power of love and nonviolence to stop its evil actions. I concluded that only violent revolution could work and that it was time to take action to make it work.

I was overseas, and I came home intending to join the underground, intending to become a revolutionary. I thank God, the Goddess or blind fate that I was recovering from malaria and pneumonia, so I was too sick to take action. To fill my time while I waited for my body to strengthen, I became a counselor at a crisis intervention center in Westport, CT. Six months later, I was no longer thinking about revolution; I was too involved in healthy, constructive activities. But I know the rage that moves

First Sunday

people to violent acts. I can relate to that feeling in the people who did this.

I do not know for certain who carried out this act, I do not know for certain what their reasoning was, but I know that like us today, they were responding to perceived injustice; like us today, they were tempted to place blame. They must have been enraged and must have blamed America for their anger, and so they engaged in acts that killed innocent people.

They were wrong. They were deeply and sadly misled, so misled that they succumbed to evil. But let us recognize that as long as there are people in this world who are oppressed; as long as there are people in this world who are victims of injustice, as long as there are people in this world who feel that their cries for justice are ignored, there will be people in this world who are willing to use violence to redress that injustice.

If we were to hunt down and kill every terrorist who is alive today, we would not end terrorism. We cannot end terrorism unless we end the conditions that create terrorists. And we cannot end terrorism if WE succumb to evil and use terrorism in response.

And so, as difficult as it is, I feel compassion for the perpetrators of these acts. I recognize in them the anger that so lives in me now, and in my nation. I caution us not to yield to the same insanity, the same burning for vengeance that might cause us to act in evil as they did.

Sometimes, when faced with events of such vast immensity, people feel paralyzed, helpless. They feel paralyzed by shock and by fear.

Our Universalist and Unitarian forebears believed that it is our duty to build the world that is to be, that we are the hands of God, of the Cosmos, of the world.

As the shock passes, we must begin to DO. But do what? There are a few steps we can begin to take:

Write letters. If you hope that the American response will be measured and careful, that we do nothing to continue the cycle of violence and revenge, write to President Bush.

Send donations; give money to those organizations working to care for the victims of this sad horror. Comfort your children. Listen to them, tell them they are safe, teach them tolerance. But most of all, express your love to them. They need to hear it. And so do adults.

Express your love. The events of Tuesday remind us that each time we see someone or take our leave from them may be the last time that we can tell them we love them. Let us do so. Tell the people that you love that you love them.

First Sunday

And let us remember what is really important in life, not just today, but always.

Those twin towers were pillars of the American financial administration. What does money mean today to the families who have lost someone? Remember what is REALLY important.

Spiritually, reach into your own faith, your own belief system, to comfort yourself and others. Pray, reflect, meditate, send good thoughts, emanate love.

These events have so shaken the confidence of many of us that we have a sense of fear and insecurity about our very lives. How do we deal with that?

There is a movement called Sufis, who represent the mystical tradition within Islam.

I am reminded of a story from the Sufi tradition where a boat is at sea, and a terrible storm comes up which terrifies the occupants of the boat, they are afraid they will founder and drown. There is a Sufi on board, and he is sitting calmly, enjoying a piece of fruit that he is eating. People near him say "How can you be so calm when the only thing between us and death is this fragile wooden hull?"; and the Sufi responds, "Is that right? Usually there is so much less between us and death.

And there is the Zen story of the Buddhist monk who falls off a steep cliff. As he is falling he grabs hold of a root sticking out of the cliff. He hangs there suspended over death. He cannot go up, and if he falls he will die. Then he sees, growing out of a crack in the cliff wall, a strawberry plant; and on it is a ripe strawberry. He picks the strawberry, takes a bite, and says "that is the most delicious strawberry I have ever tasted.

One point of these stories, I believe, is that no matter how long we live, be it 125 years, our life is just a brief flash in the eternity of time. We are all headed for death. In every moment of life we should be grateful for the fact that we HAVE life, for the astonishing miracle that we are alive and are alive now, in this moment.

Thich Nhat Hanh, the Buddhist monk, wrote of how a toothache gave him enlightenment. He said that until he had a toothache, he did not know how wonderful it was not to have a toothache. Now, everyday, he is grateful for his non-toothache. Today, whatever else has happened in our lives, no matter how much we mourn the loss of life and the destruction that has taken place, let us each be grateful for the non-death of someone we love. And let us take this brief opportunity called life to TELL them that we love them, to SHOW them that we love them, to appreciate within ourselves the fact that we love them.

Today, I am grateful to be alive. I had a really bad dinner a

First Sunday

few nights ago; three of us cooked it together, and that may have been part of the problem. Normally I would have been disappointed, even upset. But not after the events of this week; this week, as I was eating it, I was grateful to have food to eat; I was grateful to be able to eat; I was grateful to be alive to eat, and I was grateful to be with others who were eating.

May our gratitude for life override our fear and our anger.

This event is the worst thing some individuals have ever suffered. And we ought to remember to comfort and support them in their time of grief.

But we need to remember that this is not the worst thing our nation has ever suffered. The nation will go on. Our lives will go on. There will be changes, but that is part of the nature of life. Like the cycles of the seasons, like our slow slipping into autumn, there will be change. Some of those changes may be good ones. Perhaps humanity, in response to this sad, painful event, will become more united than ever before. Perhaps this moment of evil will cause us to fully recognize the interconnectedness of all the people on this planet.

Perhaps we will begin to recognize that whenever another human being is suffering, we are all called to respond.

Time will pass, and the immediate sense of shock and grief

will pass. It will take longer for some than for others. But it will pass.

Our lives will return to some semblance of normality.

This morning, before the first service, my brother came here and showed me the sonograms of my yet to be born nephew. He is due to be born on February 14. It was a moment of joy, a moment of reminder that life goes on.

Tomorrow night is Rosh Hashanah, the Jewish New Year, and many of us will gather here to welcome it in. Rosh Hashanah marks the rebirth of the world. The rebirth of the world. And so it will have special meaning for me this year, and perhaps for all of us.

May we be reminded that ever and again, as surely as autumn turns to winter and then to spring, the time of rebirth and renewal will come. Renewal will come; in its own time - in our own time, when we are ready - it will come. Have faith, yield not to fear, yield not to anger, and know that the light will return. The light WILL return.

First Sunday

Rev. Benjamin R. Doolittle

East Pearl Street Church
New Haven, Connecticut

Sunday, September 16, 2001

I was a resident physician working as a part-time pastor in an inner-city neighborhood. Since New Haven is only a few hours from Manhattan, we were all placed on alert, anticipating that hundreds of patients would be transferred to Yale-New Haven Hospital. No patients came. Slowly, we realized it was because there were no survivors: a sobering testament to how the world had changed.

My hope in the sermon was to articulate the stunned grief we all shared and then place our grief in the context of our faith. Watching the image of the billowing smoke, I kept thinking about the line from John, "And the light shines in the darkness and the darkness has no overcome it…." In the same way, Christ's departing promise because the bedrock upon which we could stand and build anew, "I am with you always even unto the end of the age." These two lines became the recurring echo for the sermon. What else could we do but stand in faith and seek the light?

The members of East Pearl St UMC always had a strong faith, a persevering faith. There was grief, for sure, but no anger towards Muslims or people from the Middle East. Our church is in a rough neighborhood, and so we know violence well. And yet, it seemed the whole world became a rough neighborhood. In response to all this, we made a "peace banner". We wrote prayers on slips of paper and pinned them to a long string. The prayers fluttered in the breeze in front of our church. We also invited folks to write their own prayers and pin them to our line. We wanted to do something immediate and tangible that there were Christians who did not hate, but were dedicated to peace. I am forever touched by the grace and compassion by which the members of East Pearl St. UMC responded to 9-11.

We are still at war. My children are 8 and 5 years old. They were not alive during 9-11, and yet 9-11 is their inheritance. They have never been alive during a time of peace in our country. I fear that war has become too matter-of-fact, too much a part of the backdrop of our lives, that we do not feel war's sting in the same way. War has become the way of life and peace is the exception. How much longer can this go on?

Light in the Land of Darkness

I Timothy 1:12-17 Luke 15:1-10

Holy, Powerful God, Our nation is at war with an enemy we cannot see, whose whereabouts we do not know. Guide us, as Christians, as a nation, to do your will. Use these words and our meditations to fortify us in the faith. In

First Sunday

Christ's name, Amen.

First, there is disbelief. Driving to the hospital. Getting bits and pieces working in the Emergency Room. A snatch of words from a reporter on the radio. A quick blurb on CNN. The disbelief increases. What happened? The World Trade Center? Did she say it was gone? The disbelief turns to mind-numbing shock. And then the shock turns to grief and an overwhelming, flooding feeling of helplessness and violation. No place is safe. And there is nothing I can do about it. I want to break something! To smash someone! To strike out! To bomb something! But where? And how? And who? I want to crawl up in a cave and never come out! I want to live as a hermit. I never want to watch the news, never want to talk to anyone ever again. World, O World, don't bother me!

Crushed. Overwhelmed. Numb. Frozen. Blown away by grief.

O God, O God, where are you? Why have you forsaken us? My heart cries out to you. My soul flees to you. But where are you when our country needs you most? When I need you most?

My God, my God, why have your forsaken us? What evil, bone-crushing, fiery, devilish evil! Where are you? The world cries out to you, even those who do not know you. And then, we, as a people, as a nation, try to look busy. We watch CNN, give blood, discuss, speculate. We watch CNN, trying to find meaning - where is God in all this? - and we get news, more speculation.

We dig in the rubble, searching for our broken heart, searching for our God. This is us, now.

But this is what I believe to be true about God, where God is in all of this. Also, this is where I believe we stand.

"In the beginning was the Word and the Word was with God, and the word was God. He was in the beginning with God. All things came into being through him, and without him not one thing came into being. What was come into being in him was life, and the life was the light of all people? The light shines in the darkness and the darkness does not overcome it."

"The light shines in the darkness and the darkness does not overcome it."

And Jesus came to his disciples, after his resurrection, and said, "All authority in heaven and on earth has been given to me. Go and make disciples of all nations . . .. And remember, I am with you always even unto the end of the age."

"And remember, I am with you always, even unto the end of the age."

First Sunday

Our nation has aimed its guns at Osama Bin Laden. Things will become more difficult before they become easier. There will be fighting and backlash. Our lives will become more vulnerable, before they become more secure. Our faith will be tested.

The evil is very great, and the darkness is very dark.

The evil that has touched East Timor, India, Kuwait, Paris, Milan, Atlanta, South Africa has touched us. We are vulnerable, exposed, naked to the violence and hatreds of the world. We now know, all too well, that we live in a fallen world.

But we are Christians. Mightier than the violence, stronger than the hatreds, is our faith. Our bodies might be crushed, but our faith is not. Our faith can heal. Our hearts may be broken, but our faith is not. Our faith can heal.

"The light shines in the darkness and the darkness does not overcome it." "And remember, I am with you always, even unto the end of the age."

We are Christians. There are many important things to do. We must give our blood. We are asked to raise our fists. We shall buy war bonds, send flashlights and batteries, bandages, and canned goods.

Donald Robert Elton & Aura Agudo Elton

Most importantly, we are Christians and we shall pray. We shall pray for justice. We shall pray for God's will to be done. We shall pray for a swift peace. We shall pray for God's Kingdom to fully come.

What the world seeks on CNN - comfort and resolve - we know already in our hearts. "The light shines in the darkness and the darkness does not overcome it." "And remember, I am with you always, even unto the end of the age." Our faith will see us through. Our God will see us through.

Let us pray,

First Sunday

Rev. Keith Grogg

Carolina Beach Presbyterian Church
Carolina Beach, North Carolina

Sunday, September 12, 2010

The sick feeling in the pit of our stomach was particular to that terrible week. I feel confident of this for two reasons; one, I had never felt exactly that way before; and two, nine years later, the commemorations and the revisiting of those first sermons after the attack brought back a memory of that exact feeling. I considered, early on, that it might heal some of our sense of helplessness in the face of such cruelty to emphasize how much had not changed. For all the weeks after the event, I stayed with the lectionary readings, trying to project a sense that no terrorist could supersede the authority of our established liturgical pattern.

The weekend of the ninth anniversary, I phoned the Imam of a local Islamic Center, my friend Abdul Shareef, and with no hesitation, he and I agreed to exchange blessings for our congregations. He read mine to his flock on the last day of Ramadan, which was Friday. Saturday was the 11th. I read his blessing on our congregation at the close of our Sunday worship services, the same Sunday that I delivered this sermon, which revisits that painful week and still seeks to witness, however poorly articulated, to the shards of hope that may still be found amid the ruins of that day.

Hope Amid the Ruins

Luke 15:1-10; I Timothy 1:12-17; Jeremiah 4:11-12, 22-27
Jeremiah 4:11-12, 22-28

11 At that time it will be said to this people and to Jerusalem: A hot wind comes from me out of the bare heights in the desert toward my poor people, not to winnow or cleanse— 12 a wind too strong for that. Now it is I who speak in judgment against them. 22 "For my people are foolish, they do not know me; they are stupid children, they have no understanding. They are skilled in doing evil, but do not know how to do good." 23 I looked on the earth, and lo, it was waste and void; and to the heavens, and they had no light. 24 I looked on the mountains, and lo, they were quaking, and all the hills moved to and fro. 25 I looked, and lo, there was no one at all, and all the birds of the air had fled. 26 I looked, and lo, the fruitful land was a desert, and all its cities were laid in ruins before the Lord, before his fierce anger. 27 For thus says the Lord: The whole land shall be a desolation; yet I will not make a full end. 28 Because of this the earth shall mourn, and the heavens above grow black; for I have spoken, I have purposed; I have not relented nor will I turn back.

First Sunday

Luke 15:1-10

1 Now all the tax collectors and sinners were coming near to listen to him. 2 And the Pharisees and the scribes were grumbling and saying, "This fellow welcomes sinners and eats with them." 3 So he told them this parable: 4 "Which one of you, having a hundred sheep and losing one of them, does not leave the ninety-nine in the wilderness and go after the one that is lost until he finds it? 5 When he has found it, he lays it on his shoulders and rejoices. 6 And when he comes home, he calls together his friends and neighbors, saying to them, 'Rejoice with me, for I have found my sheep that was lost.' 7 Just so, I tell you, there will be more joy in heaven over one sinner who repents than over ninety-nine righteous persons who need no repentance. 8 "Or what woman having ten silver coins, if she loses one of them, does not light a lamp, sweep the house, and search carefully until she finds it? 9 When she has found it, she calls together her friends and neighbors, saying, 'Rejoice with me, for I have found the coin that I had lost.' 10 Just so, I tell you, there is joy in the presence of the angels of God over one sinner who repents." 11 Then Jesus said, "There was a man who had two sons. 12 The younger of them said, 'Father, give me the share of the property that will belong to me.' So he divided his property between them. 13 A few days later the younger son gathered all he had and traveled to a distant country, and there he squandered his property in dissolute living. 14 When he had spent everything, a severe famine took place

throughout that country, and he began to be in need. 20 So he set off and went to his father. But while he was still far off, his father saw him and was filled with compassion; he ran and put his arms around him and kissed him [and said], 'Let us eat and celebrate; 24 for this son of mine was dead and is alive again; he was lost and is found!' And they began to celebrate.

I Timothy 1:12-17

12 I am grateful to Christ Jesus our Lord, who has strengthened me, because he judged me faithful and appointed me to his service, 13 even though I was formerly a blasphemer, a persecutor, and a man of violence. But I received mercy because I had acted ignorantly in unbelief, 14 and the grace of our Lord overflowed for me with the faith and love that are in Christ Jesus. 15 The saying is sure and worthy of full acceptance, that Christ Jesus came into the world to save sinners—of whom I am the foremost. 16 But for that very reason I received mercy, so that in me, as the foremost, Jesus Christ might display the utmost patience, making me an example to those who would come to believe in him for eternal life. 17 To the King of the ages, immortal, invisible, the only God, be honor and glory forever and ever. Amen.

A light shines in the darkness, and the darkness did not overcome it.

First Sunday

"We know," Paul famously wrote to the church in Rome, "that all things work together for good for those who love God."

It's a daring statement, but Paul would know. As an observant Jew, he was familiar with both the history and the promise of the people of God.

The history included the destruction of Jerusalem at the hands of the Babylonians. 600 years before Christ, Nebuchadnezzar, with his massive Babylonian army, sacked the Temple in Jerusalem, took valuables but left the structure intact. Ten years later, he came back to finish the job. They leveled Jerusalem; they burned the Temple to the ground; they took away the best and the brightest among Israel's population, and the rest scattered, and that was the beginning of the Babylonian Exile—an unparalleled, unmitigated national disaster. They didn't lose God, but they lost everything they knew, everything they thought they had understood about life and the world and their place in it.

So how to explain such destruction among the people of God? Well, look at the prophecy of Jeremiah just before the fall of Jerusalem.

Despite all that God had done for them, God's people either stubbornly refused to reflect that awesome reality in their lives, or they just, in the midst of their good times and their challenges, found it all too easy to live for themselves and forget about God and their fellow human beings: And Jeremiah, like so many prophets before him, tried to get the people's attention, and looking toward God's judgment, he said with a harshness rarely seen in the Bible:

"It will be said to this people and to Jerusalem: A hot wind comes from me out of the bare heights in the desert toward my poor people, not to winnow or cleanse—a wind too strong for that. Now it is I who speak in judgment against them.

"For my people are foolish, they do not know me; they are stupid children, they have no understanding. They are skilled in doing evil, but do not know how to do good." And the result, according to the Old Testament, was the leveling of Jerusalem and the scattering of God's people. So when Paul, a descendant of those people, said, "We know that all things work together for good for those who love God," he knew the gravity of what he was saying.

But he also knew the promise of the covenant people, the promise inherent in God's unsurpassable love for them.

The promise was that they were and always would be God's covenant people, a covenant through which the salvation of all creation would be mediated.

The promise is that there is no circumstance so awful, no

First Sunday

amount of wreckage or carnage so disheartening, that God cannot draw up from it redemption and promise and hope. A light shines in the darkness, and the darkness did not overcome it.

Nine years ago yesterday, a calamity struck, of a magnitude which most of us never thought we would see.

A few weeks later, on World Communion Sunday, even as we were still dealing with our collective and individual sense of deep woundedness and loss, we could already see that out of the horror, and the destruction, and the fear, something else had happened.

Those of us who are old enough will always remember being able to stop and think:

Just for a little while, didn't we feel a little bit closer to the people around us? Weren't we, just for a minute, a little more united? Wasn't there a selflessness that pervaded this country?

Weren't we saying things to each other that we couldn't have imagined we'd ever be saying to other people, about how much we valued them, how much we needed and loved them?

And didn't a lot of people in other countries who had a beef with the United States ignore that fact for just a few days, while they somehow got ahold of American flags and held them high, out of respect and sympathy?

I saw German firefighters with their heads bowed and their helmets in their hands. I saw Hispanic people in Central America, Arab people in Northern Africa, Asian people in the far East, people of all colors in Africa, North America, Europe, and around the world, standing united, when if they hadn't wanted to, they wouldn't have had to.

And didn't it make a little more sense for a few days—and wasn't it a little more directly to the point—that when the things that symbolized my power, my identity, my life, and my security seemed to be taken from me, when the burning towers of my fragile existence were collapsing, Jesus gave up his own life, and never looked back when it was time to put on his uniform and go into the collapsing wreckage to save me?

Here in Luke's gospel, the stories he told made it clear what he intended to do for us and he wasn't talking to his faithful disciples or the adoring crowd; he was talking to his enemies, his doubters, the ones who were disgusted by his habit of reaching out to outcasts and sinners and anyone who would listen.
He told three stories: about a shepherd going out of his way to come to the rescue of one lost sheep, even when 99 others were still right where they needed to be.

First Sunday

He told about a woman who searches and searches for a missing coin, turning the house upside down until she finds it, as if that coin alone was worth as much as the other nine that were safely accounted for.

He told about a father whose son had betrayed everything he stood for and walked away from it all, caring for no one but himself; but when that son came back home destitute, that father ran and hugged him and threw a huge party because he was so happy to have his son back, safe at home, just like the other one who had never left the father's side.

Whether you are one of a hundred, or one of ten, or one of two, you are so important to God that no kind of devastation, no amount of straying that you do, can ever keep God from seeking you out, valuing you, loving you as much as God loves anyone else among God's children.

And so, Paul said,

"I am grateful to Christ Jesus our Lord, because he judged me faithful and appointed me to his service, even though I was a blasphemer, a persecutor, and a man of violence. But his grace overflowed for me with faith and love.

"The saying is sure and worthy of full acceptance, that Christ Jesus came into the world to save sinners—and no one," said Paul, "no one was more of a sinner than I.

"And that is exactly why I received mercy: so that in me, as the foremost sinner, Jesus Christ might display the utmost patience, making me an example to everyone who would come to believe in him for eternal life."

No matter who you are or what your circumstances, no matter how lost and afraid you may find yourself, no matter who you have been or what you have done, no matter the scale of the destruction all around you, Christ Jesus came into the world to save.

To the King of the ages, immortal, invisible, the only God, be honor and glory forever and ever.

Amen.

First Sunday

Rev. John Hamby

First Baptist Church
Vilonia, AR

September 8, 2002

Introduction to the 9-11 Service

President Bush has declared September 9th through the 11th as National Days of Prayer and Remembrance. It is in Light of that declaration we have set today aside as a congregation to lead us into that time of prayer and remembrance. We will begin our service this morning by repeating the "Pledge of Allegiance" but we do so not just as an act of patriotism but to remind us that we are indeed "one nation under God." In June, a federal court created a national uproar when it ruled the Pledge unconstitutional because it contained the words "One nation under God." The courts will not decide if this is one nation under God," we as a people decide that every day by the choices we make. Would you stand with me as Bro. Scott comes to lead us in the "Pledge of Allegiance?"

Remembering the Tragedy of 9-11

Some events in human history impact us so greatly that we will forever have engraved in our minds where we were and what we were doing when we heard the news. I'll never forget that I was sitting in my sixth grade classroom when we heard the news that the President of the United States, John F. Kennedy had been assassinated. Nor will I forget stepping out from taking a shower in a motel room in Fayetteville, Arkansas and hearing Bro. Brian tell me that he thought someone had just flown an airplane into one of the Twin Towers in New York. As I sat down on edge of the bed to find out more details, I watched in horror as the second plane crashing into the South Tower. Those images are forever embedded in my memory. You no doubt remember exactly where you were and what you were doing when you first heard the news.

Our president has called for National Days of Prayer and Remembrance, but what is it that we should remember?

We Need To Remember The Cost In Human Lives.

On September 11th, nearly 3,000 people lost their lives at the World Trade Center, the Pentagon and in rural fields in Pennsylvania. It was the most devastating attack ever to happen on American soil; costing more lives than even the attack on Pearl Harbor (2,500 Americans died then) Nineteen cowardly individuals, who killed in the name of religion, carried out this insidious attack).
We need to be careful not to forget the lives that were lost on that dreadful day and not to forget the lives of those

who have been forever changed. Not to forget the widows who are raising children alone. Not to forget the parents who will never hold their children again

We Need To Remember The Extraordinary Acts Of Heroism And Compassion

We also need to not forget the heroism shown by ordinary people who rose to the occasion in extraordinary ways. Reactions to this crisis, has brought forth both the best and the worse in people. Yes, there have been some dark spots such as the Pakistani woman who was purposefully run down while crossing a supermarket lot with groceries simply because she wore the traditional dress of her homeland. But it has also called forth unnumbered heroic acts, some recorded and many that were not. There were many lights in the darkness.

September 11th shocked this nation, and in remembering that tragic day: let us gain a renewed respect for those who have proven themselves to be true heroes! The firefighters, police, and rescue workers who risked their lives and even gave their lives to save others are true heroes!

One thing September 11 has shown us is that we never know…none of us ever know how much time we have—or how much time those around us have…therefore it is imperative that we spread the news of the saving Gospel of Christ with everyone we can!

The last issue of the "Focus on the Family Magazine," [Christin Ditchfield. September 2002. "A Light In the Darkness." pages 18-19] detailed the actions of Al Braca. Al worked on the 105th floor of Tower One. When he realized that they were trapped in the building and would be unable to escape, Al shared the gospel with 50 of his coworkers and led them in prayer. Some of those same individuals had in the past mocked him for his faith.

If September 11 can teach us anything.... anything good at all...certainly it shows us that by following the model of Christ....ordinary Christians like you and me can be heroes!!!

And who hasn't heard of the heroic act of the passengers aboard United Airlines Flight 93? One of those passengers was named Todd Beamer, in a conversation with a telephone operator he told that plane had been hijacked and that the passengers were discussing ways to overpower the hijackers. He ended his conversation by asking the operator to pray with him. The last words the operator heard him say were "Are you guys ready, Lets Roll." The heroic sacrificial action by those passengers to bring down the plane no doubt saved many lives as the hijackers were denied their ultimate target. Some have suggested its target was the White House and the President of the United

First Sunday

States. [Tom Neven. Focus on the Family Magazine. "Lets Roll" pages 2-4]

One story was told of an American reaching across religious and ethic lines to help. One such story was told by a Pakistani man named Usman Farman, he worked in building #7 of the World Trade Center. He was one of the luck ones who made it out of the building, when he saw the collapse of the first building he began to run. In the process he fell on his back on the ground and looked on as a massive cloud of debris was overtaking him. At that moment an orthodox Jewish man came up to him, and saw the Muslim pendant he wore around his neck, a prayer for safety. He held it in his hand and read out loud in Arabic for a second and then in a Brooklyn accent he said, "Brother if you don't mind, there is a cloud of glass coming at us, grab my hand and lets get the hell out of here. Farman said "He was the last person I would have thought would have helped me.' ["Brother if you don't mind." www.e46fanatics.com]

What We Need To Remember Islam Is Not Just Another Denomination

The Media has made much of reporting on the religion of Islam. Perhaps in an attempt to get people not to react negatively to Moslem in this country, an effort has been made to normalize the adherents to Islam. But let's not be confused. Islam is not just another denomination. Islam is not like the Methodist down the street or the new

Assembly of God starting up here in town. Just because they worship one God does not mean that it is same God. In a future message I intend to address the issue that "Allah is Not Our God," but suffice it to say today, that although everyone has the freedom to worship as they see fit in this country, we do not, nor should we, accept that Allah is just another name for Jehovah.

We Need To Remember What This Has Revealed To Us About State Of The Church

Perhaps most distressing of all is what this crisis has revealed about our country's relationship with God. Immediately after the attacks, church attendance spiked for several weeks, rising in some places to as much as half the regular adult attendance. That attendance surge was short-lived though, for levels were back to normal by November. Much as they did after the Gulf War. I have even heard some suggest that they were lower than prior to Sept 11. George Barna the church statistician, professed his amazement saying, " I was among those who fully expected to see an intense spiritual reaction to the terrorist attacks. The fact that we saw no lasting impact from the most significant act of war against our country on our own soil says something about the spiritual complacency of the American public." [Barna Research Online. "Half of All Adults Say Their Faith Helped Them Personally Handle the 9-11 Aftermath" www.barna.org]

First Sunday

He went on to say that he felt that the influx was due to irregulars (those who attend once every month or two) suddenly returning on a consistent basis for a month or so, before they fell back into their "regular pattern of irregular attendance."

We Need To Be Reminded Of Where To Look For Our Strength (Psalm 46)

God is our refuge and strength, A very present help in trouble.(2) Therefore we will not fear, Even though the earth be removed, And though the mountains be carried into the midst of the sea; (3) Though its waters roar and be troubled, Though the mountains shake with its swelling. (4) There is a river whose streams shall make glad the city of God, The holy place of the tabernacle of the Most High. (5) God is in the midst of her, she shall not be moved; God shall help her, just at the break of dawn. (6) The nations raged, the kingdoms were moved; He uttered His voice, the earth melted. (7) The LORD of hosts is with us; The God of Jacob is our refuge. .... (10) Be still, and know that I am God; I will be exalted among the nations, I will be exalted in the earth! (11) The LORD of hosts is with us; The God of Jacob is our refuge."

In this psalm David encourages believers in times of trouble. Psalm 46 is famous as the inspiration of Martin Luther's great Hymn "A Mighty Fortress Is Our God."

When David said, "God is our refuge" what he meant was that our sense of security is not derived from our nations defenses but that it rests in our faith in God. God and God alone is our refuge in times such as these. As believers we need to remember that our feeling of security goes beyond the measures of home land defense, beyond metal detectors, security checks, military power, political alliances or the strength of our economy. Our faith must rest solidly on a relationship with a living God. Security is not the absence of trouble, but the presence of confidence and courage in the midst of trouble. When tragedy occurs there are tears. Tears of those directly affected and tears of sympathy.

David reminds us that God is not only or refuge but our "strength." Strength is the ability to rise above tragedy even with tears in our eyes and go forward. God is not just some far off source from whom we can seek advice but this psalm tells us that he is "a very present help."

David ends this great psalm by reminding us in verse ten that it is when we are overwhelmed that we need to allow God to move. "Be still, and know that I am God; I will be exalted among the nations, I will be exalted in the earth! (11) The LORD of hosts is with us; The God of Jacob is our refuge."

The Twin Towers have been destroyed and with them

First Sunday

symbols of America's security and prosperity. But beyond all the tragedy and the tears, the terror and the fears, one symbol still stands strong it is the cross.

Conclusion

God was not surprised by 9-11
But He was saddened by it.
God did not cause 9-11
But He does comfort those affected by It.
God may not choose to prevent future acts of terrorism
But He will provide peace in the hearts of all those who turn to Him.

At times such as this, more than anything else, I believe that we need to be reminded that God cares! The Bible reveals to us that God does indeed care. The Philips translation of I Peter 5:7 says, "You can throw the whole weight of your anxieties on him, for you are his personal concern." The Living Bible paraphrases that verse with these words, "Let him have all your worries and cares, for he is always thinking about you and watching everything that concerns you." It is comforting to know that God is aware of your feelings today and desires to comfort you.

Rev. John A. Huffman, Jr.

St. Andrews Presbyterian Church
Newport Beach, CA

Saturday, September 15, 2001

My wife Anne and I had been in Europe for a couple of weeks and flew home on Monday, September 10 from Rome to Orange County by way of Brussels, and Chicago. We apparently were the last flight into Orange County carrying anyone returning from Europe. Early the next morning I took a long walk to help recover from jet lag only to walk into the family room as Anne and my daughter Janet shouted 'A plane just crashed into the World Trade Center, come see the replay...' only to discover it was not a replay but the second plane being carried live on T.V. as it also crashed into one of the buildings. From that moment on I did nothing but watch and read everything I could about this act of terrorism while at the same time writing down observations and various Scripture texts that would ultimately become the major elements of the sermon. In the process, at my daughter Janet's insistence, we made plans for a community service that Friday night. I was amazed at the cross-section of the community that showed up including the head of the local Islamic Center and some of his members. He asked for the opportunity to address the people who were coming and going over the time of this extended memorial service. I let him do so and he humbly apologized for what had happened and begged us

First Sunday

to understand that this was an aberration, not the result of historic Islamic teaching. The Saturday night and Sunday morning worship services were extremely well attended. There was great attention given to what I had to say by both our regular attendees and the many more who for some reason were drawn to church by the incident.

However, this soon wore off and life pretty much went back to normal within a few weeks. And a course of political action was set that opened the door to massive fear and the military ventures into Afghanistan and Iraq. The overwhelming spiritual interest which momentarily emerged seemed to pretty much evaporate. My prayer is that my message and those of many other pastors bore some long range spiritual fruit. Only God knows what that was! Church life settled back into normalcy very quickly.

Response to Crisis: A Biblical Perspective for Our National Tragedy
Psalms 55:1-23

Cast your cares on the Lord and he will sustain you; he will never let the righteous fall. But you, O God, will bring down the wicked into the pit of corruption; bloodthirsty and deceitful men will not live out half their days. But as for me, I trust in you. (Psalm 55:22-23)

When did you hear and where were you when you heard Tuesday morning? You'll probably never forget! Anne and

Donald Robert Elton & Aura Agudo Elton

I had just returned from Europe Monday evening. Unbeknownst to us, we were among the last to make it home, as in that one long day we flew from Rome to Brussels, Brussels to Chicago, and Chicago into Orange County Airport.

I've discovered the best way to fight jet lag is to exercise. So I got up early Tuesday morning to take my aerobic walk, took a bit longer route than usual, smarting from the pain of having been pick-pocketed in the Rome subway Sunday night and having had my luggage lost on Monday. I usually make it home from my walk to catch the 7 o'clock news on the Today show. But I consciously thought, It's been a slow news summer. I've heard all I want to hear about Gary Condit, and an extra fifteen minutes of exercise before our first staff retreat of the year would be of greater value than the top of the news.

When I arrived home at 7:20 a.m. I was surprised to see both Janet and Anne riveted to the television. As they tried to tell me something, I saw an airliner crash into a building. I then saw another instant replay. At that moment I, like you, became riveted to the news, obsessed with our national tragedy. Everything else, including stolen wallets filled with cash, credit cards, drivers licenses, family pictures and other valuables, along with a suitcase stuffed full of clothes and personal affects, seemed incidental to the horrendous loss of life and shock to our American psyche.

First Sunday

I must admit that after a half hour of watching those outrageously bizarre events with those four planes crashing, I wondered if the commentators would stop and sheepishly declare that this was a contemporary update of the old Orson Welles' "invasion of the planet" deception of decades ago and it would be revealed that this was a computerized simulation of a fictional terrorist attack meant to momentarily shock the nation, and then relieve us as we discovered our vulnerability to such technological trickery. But no such announcement was made. And the horror settled in as all air flights were canceled, key government buildings were evacuated, and for a while we did not even know the whereabouts of our President.

I don't know how close you've come to a personal connect with this tragedy. We've all empathized with the stories of passengers having those touching last phone conversations with loved ones. We've witnessed the relief of those who would have been on those planes or in those towers but for some reason were delayed. We've been amazed at the stories of those who made their way down ninety floors, escaping all injury, and one who even apparently fell a great distance in the implosion, coming out relatively unscathed. Then the dark side is filled with the horror of business firms who lost hundreds of employees, families that are shattered, and even the tragic story of a child who lost one parent, a passenger in the plane, and the other parent who worked in the Trade Center.

Donald Robert Elton & Aura Agudo Elton

Yes, there has been a quantum change in the way we, as Americans, look at life. Never again will we live in a perception of isolation that has given us such security in the past. Those horror stories of distant terrorist bombings in the Middle East where U.S. embassies were blown up in Dar-Es-salaam, Tanzania or Nairobi, Kenya have now come close to home. The federal office building devastation of Oklahoma City, which seemed like such an isolated aberration, becomes a simple precursor to this week's fast-moving events that put our whole nation on alert. As one building after another crumbled in New York, the Pentagon continued to burn in Arlington, Virginia. Even the White House became vulnerable.

As we watched that Friday noon service of prayer and remembrance in the National Cathedral, as representatives of all faiths participated, our national leadership gathered in that one house of worship, and as we listened to a frail, elderly Billy Graham speak with such great biblical insight into the moment, I could not help but become convinced that our American preoccupation with entertainment was going to seem increasingly shallow. Worship services that are human-centered and preaching that is appreciated for the standup comedic gifts of the communicator will no longer carry the day as one insightful writer has reflected -- we are a nation of people who are "amusing ourselves to death." I doubt that we'll be able to do that any longer. Oh certainly, Jay Leno and David Letterman will be back in

First Sunday

business in a few days. And God help us if we completely lose our sense of humor.

But, frankly, what you and I need is a biblical perspective, a Word from God to help us face the national tragedy at the present and its implications for the future. So let me share with you some biblical insights that are God-given to help us cope, as hurting men and women endeavoring to face the reality of our own questions in a broken, hurting world.

Insight one: At the deepest level, all life is filled with mystery. Be wary of any human leader who claims to have all the answers, myself included.

I, and people like me -- your pastors, teachers, theologians, philosophers -- will and should wrestle with the deepest issues of life. But remember what the Apostle Paul wrote in 1 Corinthians 13:9-12: For we know in part and we prophesy in part, but when perfection comes, the imperfect disappears. When I was a child, I talked like a child, I thought like a child, I reasoned like a child. When I became a man, I put childish ways behind me. Now we see but a poor reflection as in a mirror; then we shall see face to face. Now I know in part; then I shall know fully, even as I am fully known.

God is the only one who understands. And even He has His heart broken by what He sees.

Donald Robert Elton & Aura Agudo Elton

Each of us views life from our own limited perspective. We react on instincts developed over a lifetime of handling the expected and the unexpected. And we all crave answers.

That's why the churches have been so full this week and why entertainment-oriented talk shows and sporting events have been canceled or postponed. There's something in each of us that in moments of tragedy opens up yearning for an eternal perspective, a divine insight, that makes some kind of sense out of life in all of its confusion.

My 26-year-old-daughter, Janet, confronted me with this reality. Wednesday evening, Anne, Janet and I had a quiet dinner on the tenth anniversary of our daughter Suzanne's death. Our other daughter, Carla, was going to join us, but all flights had been cancelled and she could not get here from Seattle for our evening of commemoration. Even as the three of us were musing on the mystery of Suzanne's death at age 23, Janet suddenly looked at me and said, "Dad, why isn't St. Andrew's having a special service in honor of the national tragedy?"

I defensively responded, "Our chapel has been open. We're having a candlelight vigil all day for any who want to come and pray. And we've redesigned three services this weekend to concentrate on this theme."

First Sunday

"That's not enough," she responded. "People need a place to come and pray and express themselves out loud to each other." I went home and barely slept on Wednesday night, tossing and rolling until I sensed the Holy Spirit saying, "John, though the Session isn't meeting again, you're the pastor. Announce the service, 5 to 7 p.m. on Friday, where people can come and simply pray and hear the Scriptures read, express themselves, and perhaps even sing a hymn or two in a candlelight vigil."

I came to the church Thursday morning, announced it, and only later discovered that Friday had been set aside as a day for prayer and remembrance. I was stunned to see this sanctuary fill up with people at 5 o'clock. By 6 o'clock perhaps half of them had left. But almost instantly, as some would leave others would come and take their seats and their candle, and the sanctuary was still full. Many of these people I don't remember ever seeing before. We all were there seeking perspective and even answers to the mystery of terrorism and the apparent random nature of life and death.

Insight two: The God of all creation is the only one who has the answers.

Billy Graham, at the National Day of Prayer service, made one statement that, in my estimation, stands out above everything else I've heard this week. He said, "God is sovereign even in things we don't understand!"

Take this God seriously. Open His Word, the Bible. The Bible is the only infallible rule of faith and practice. Or another way of saying it is that the Bible is God's written way of communicating to you and me, as His Holy Spirit inspired the prophets and apostles of old, to tell you and me not everything about God, ourselves and each other, but enough about himself, about ourselves and each other, to get along with Him, ourselves and each other.

How sad is the person who wanders through life isolated from God, soured by life, yearning for something more, yet not realizing that that "something more" is available through a personal relationship with God in Jesus Christ.

I know it's so easy to get caught up in life that you don't take the time for daily Bible reading and prayer. I know that even when you do read the Bible, at times, it seems boring, lest we come to it with the same kind of attention that we give to our business activities, our social life, and our sailing, our tennis swing, our golf game.

By the time I got to our staff retreat at 9:30 on Tuesday morning I had not yet opened the Bible. I had sat, mesmerized, in front of the television set, then only shaved and showered just in time to make it to the meeting. With great confidence, I opened the One Year Bible. This particular version has a daily reading from the Old Testament, from the New Testament, from the Psalms,

First Sunday

from the Book of Proverbs. With great confidence, I shared with the staff, "I'm going to read from the Psalm for today, believing that God has a Word for us in our puzzlement."

Let me read the opening and closing verses:

Listen to my prayer, O God, do not ignore my plea; hear me and answer me. My thoughts trouble me and I am distraught at the voice of my enemy, at the stares of the wicked; for they bring down suffering upon me and revile me in their anger. My heart is in anguish within me; the terrors of death assail me. Fear and trembling have beset me; horror has overwhelmed me. I said, "Oh, that I had the wings of a dove! I would fly away and be at rest -- I would flee far away and stay in the desert; I would hurry to my place of shelter, far from the tempest and storm." Confuse the wicked, O Lord, confound their speech, for I see violence and strife in the city. Day and night they prowl about on its walls; malice and abuse are within it. Destructive forces are at work in the city; threats and lies never leave its streets.

(Psalm 55:1-11)
The psalm then closes with these finals words:
Cast your cares on the Lord and he will sustain you; he will never let the righteous fall. But you, O God, will bring down the wicked into the pit of corruption; bloodthirsty and deceitful men will not live out half their days. But as for me. I trust in you. (Psalm 55:22-23)

Insight three: God's truth is multidimensional and never simplistic.

There are multi-dimensions to truth, God's truth. Some of these multi-dimensions seem to be in competition with each other. We would rather see this as the dynamic tensions of truth that is not simplistic.

If you read the Bible carefully, you will see, on occasion, a call to peacemaking, which could cause one to become a pacifist. At the same time, there are other passages that call us to act decisively in military response, to crush the enemies of God and those who would bring injustice, destruction to the innocent.

There are passages that call us to turn the other cheek, forgiving our enemies, to function in dynamic tension with those passages that call us to annihilate evil, living in separation from the evil doer.

There are passages that emphasize the sovereignty of God and the fact that He is in control of the universe that exist in dynamic tension with those passages in the Bible that talk about the freedom He has given to human beings to make their own choices and to live with the positive and negative consequences of those choices as they impact us and as they impact others. You will read passages in the Bible that encourage you to see that everything God created is good and to use all He's created to celebrate life

First Sunday

existing in dynamic tension with those passages that call us to pick up our cross, follow Jesus, and live lives of self-denial.

There are Bible verses that urge us to pray for God's healing of our physical, emotional, and spiritual diseases. We have case examples of those who have been instantaneously, miraculously healed as well as those stories of men and women who lived with their "thorns in the flesh," praying for deliverance, but finding a different kind of healing than the one for which they prayed.

You take God's biblical perspective seriously and you will live with the reality that life is messy, it's not simplistic. God's truth is multidimensional. You and I legitimately raise the question, "How can a good, all-powerful God allow evil in this world?" "How could He have allowed those four planes to have crashed in those diabolical ways with such horrendous loss of life?"

I don't know. I'm human. But God does know. Isaiah declared it so succinctly when he said: Seek the Lord while he may be found; call on him while he is near. Let the wicked forsake his way and the evil man his thoughts. Let him turn to the Lord, and he will have mercy on him, and to our God, for he will freely pardon. "For my thoughts are not your thoughts, neither are your ways my ways," declares the Lord. (Isaiah 55:6-8)

Insight four: Don't be afraid to argue and even be angry with God.

God wants to have honest conversation with you. Adoration of God and reverence of Him is very important in prayer. At the same time, God does not want someone to go through phony, fake, verbal gyrations to try to win His favor. He knows our hearts. He knows our questions. He knows our anguish. He is touched with the feelings of what we feel and wants us to express ourselves honestly to Him. Just imagine how superficial would be a parent-child relationship if the child constantly flattered the parent, trying to make Mom or Dad feel good in an ongoing effort to get more gum, candy, an increase in allowance, in favored position over the other siblings. We have some unflattering labels for people who are constantly "kissing it up" to people in power positions over them. God is as nauseated with that kind of false flattery as are you and I.

There's a virility to the Psalms. Today's Psalm 55 opens with this heartfelt, demanding prayer of David: Listen to my prayer, O God, do not ignore my plea; hear me and answer me. My thoughts trouble me and I am distraught at the voice of the enemy, at the stares of the wicked; for they bring down suffering upon me and revile me in their anger. (Psalm 55:1-3)

Remember, Jesus Christ, on the cross, cried out in anguish, "My God, My God, why have you forsaken me?" You say

First Sunday

well that was God in human form, the Son of God, he's entitled having emptied himself of his divinity to, in His humanity, cry out in that demanding way.

Never forget, Jesus, on the cross, was simply quoting from that Old Testament Psalm 22 in which, once again, David cries out in a demanding, almost angry, argumentative way, these words: My God, My God, why have you forsaken me? Why are you so far from saving me, so far from the words of my groaning? O my God, I cry out by day, but you do not answer, by night, and am not silent. (Psalm 22:1-2)

God wants honest communication. The "laments" go all the way through the psalms. The questioning of God is a sign of virile faith, declaring that we are in relationship with this One, that we do take Him seriously, that we yearn for our answers, that we are able to argue with Him -- always in the context of beginning with a prayer acknowledging we are creatures and He is Creator, though, at the same time, taking Him seriously enough to engage Him in virile, vital, strong conversation.

Insight five: Accept the fact that life is not easy and that there are wicked people in this world.

Back in 1978, M. Scott Peck catapulted onto the American literary scene with his best-selling book titled The Road Less Traveled. It was labeled a "new psychology of love, traditional values and spiritual growth." I'm convinced that the key to its success was embodied in the first sentence which simply reads: "Life is difficult."

Accept that fact, and everything else sort of falls into place. We are fallen men and women living in a fallen world. The Psalmist nails it with these words: My thoughts trouble me and I am distraught at the voice of the enemy, at the stares of the wicked; for they bring down suffering upon me and revile me in their anger (Psalm 55:2-3).

There are wicked people in this world. The Psalmist is aware of it as he writes: Confuse the wicked, O Lord, confound their speech, for I see violence and strife in the city. Day and night they prowl about on its walls; malice and abuse are within it. Destructive forces are at work in the city; threats and lies never leave its streets. (Psalm 55:9-11)

Three thousand years later, it's the same thing. We shouldn't be surprised. Life is difficult. There are wicked people in this world. Sometimes the wicked person is someone else. Sometimes I'm the wicked person. More often there's a strange alchemy in which there's a mix of wickedness and goodness in both the other and in me.

That's why the Apostle Paul made it so clear in Romans 3:23 when he writes: " ... for all have sinned and fall short of the glory of God...." We are all in this boat together!

First Sunday

Insight six: Be aware of our tendency to flee to an illusionary safe place.

Tuesday morning's Los Angeles Times, prior to those ghastly plane crashes that same day, had an article describing how we here live on the Newport-Inglewood fault. We've forgotten that last Sunday there was a 4.2 earthquake that shook large parts of Los Angeles and appears to have involved the north end of the Newport-Ingle wood fault, "One of the most dangerous in Southern California," three leading quake scientists said Monday. It begins just off the Orange County coast by us and goes 50 miles northwest through Long Beach, Inglewood, and into west Los Angeles and is "capable of generating a quake in the magnitude 7 range and has been the subject of dire quake scenarios because it runs directly under some of the most densely populated areas of Southern California." Articles like that make me want to move to a safe place.

Then comes our national tragedy, and we discover that smoldering cities do not belong just to the bombings of World War I, World War II, and those countries which today are involved in wars. We, too, now are vulnerable. And my heart cries out with the Psalmist: Oh, that I had the wings of a dove! I would fly away and be at rest -- I would flee far away and stay in the desert; I would hurry to my place of shelter, far from the tempest and storm (Psalm 55:6-8).

But where is that place? You can move to Montana and find out that some crazy mail bomber is living in the cabin just down the road. And there are drugs there, too, as well as natural disasters.

I love those words of Psalm 139 which both warn the person who wants to flee from the presence of God or those of us who are desirous of getting to a safe place somewhere else. The fact is, God is with us wherever we are: Where can I go from your Spirit? Where can I flee from your presence? If I go up to the heavens, you are there; if I make my bed in the depths, you are there. If I rise on the wings of the dawn, if I settle on the far side of the sea, even there your hand will guide me, your right hand will hold me fast. (Psalm 139:7-10)

I've had friends that have uprooted and moved to the San Juan Islands or Hawaii or to that cabin in Montana. Some have come back, discovering they had fled to an illusionary haven. Others have stayed, acknowledging that there is not a more perfect place than that of being in the center of God's will, which is determined by relationship, not by place.

Insight seven: We all need each other.

President Bush, in his message yesterday at The National Cathedral, used these words to describe people sacrificially

First Sunday

helping each other: "Inside the World Trade Center, one man who could have saved himself stayed until the end and at the side of his quadriplegic friend. A beloved priest died giving the last rites to a firefighter. Two office workers, finding a disabled stranger, carried her down 68 floors to safety. A group of men drove through the night from Dallas to Washington to bring skin grafts for burned victims."

Psalm 68:6 reads: "God sets the lonely in families...." Some of us are privileged to have nuclear family -- a father, mother, brother, sister, parent, child. For some, that's never been a reality. God's given us the church, the gathered people, the family of God, where we can be in relationship with each other. That's why, instinctually, people crowd to churches looking for relationship and answers when the artificial props are pulled out from under them. Thank God for communities in which we live where we have friends and neighbors.

Galatians 6:2 reads: "Carry each other's burdens, and in this way you will fulfill the law of Christ." That's communitarian talk.

Where would we have been this week without those heroes in the New York Fire Department and Police Department? These men and women have been much maligned in recent days. How can a community function without each other? We need doctors, coaches, teachers, garbage collectors, police persons, firemen, salespersons, the waitress, school volunteers, and the list goes on.

Insight eight: Life at the longest is brief.

Tuesday morning, every one of those men and women got out of bed, dressed, went to work, went to the airport, assuming it was just a normal day in a slow news week. Few of them ever dreamed that Tuesday was the last day of their life on earth.

Look into their faces as you see them on television, as they're pictured in the newspapers. All next week we'll see them in glossy photos in the news magazines. They were vital, alive, Tuesday morning And now they're gone.

I look around this sanctuary. I see the faces of people no longer with us. Special people, valued persons of all ages, now in heaven with Jesus.
At just about every memorial service I do, I read these words from Psalm 90:

Lord, you have been our dwelling place throughout all generations. Before the mountains were born or you brought forth the earth and the world, from everlasting to everlasting you are God. (verses 1-2)

For a thousand years in your sight are like a day that has just gone by, or like a watch in the night. You sweep men

First Sunday

away in the sleep of death; they are like the new grass of the morning -- though in the morning it springs up new, by evening it is dry and withered, (verses 4-6)

The length of our days is seventy years -- or eighty, if we have the strength; yet their span is but trouble and sorrow, for they quickly pass, and we fly away. (v. 10)

Teach us to number our days aright, that we may gain a heart of wisdom, (v. 12)

May the favor of the Lord our God rest upon us; establish the work of our hands for us -- yes, establish the work of our hands, (v. 17)

In a way, all of us are living on borrowed time. Part of the grief we experience in a week like this comes from what is called "survivor's guilt." Why them, not us? Why am I alive at age sixty-one when my precious daughter died ten years ago at age twenty-three? Yet, most of us don't think of these things until a tragedy hits. Then we wallow in momentary awareness of the finite nature of our human existence, only to inoculate ourselves against it as life gets back to its ordinary pace. And it will, as the memories of this week begin to dull with the passing of time.

Insight nine: We dare not become the evil we deplore.

Donald Robert Elton & Aura Agudo Elton

There's a tendency for revenge that makes the persecuted the persecutor.

Our immediate instinct to events such as those of this week is to declare war. The only problem we have now is we do not know for certain who is the enemy. A woman called this week and asked the question, "What position does our church take on the retaliation to terrorists?" She relates how she's tried to be a voice of moderation and restraint from her Christian perspective, but family and friends raise the question, "How can you think like that?" Her own father declares, "We should just bomb them." The question is, "Who is the 'them?'"

Afghanistan is an impoverished nation. I've been there. They've been in a decade war against Russia, followed by a decade of civil war, the last four years of which have been a drought bringing an increased devastation on an already impoverished nation. This terrorist threat is much more sophisticated, than this historic warfare between nations. There are underground, anonymous cells right here in our own country. We wouldn't think of dropping a bomb on a block in Brooklyn or a suburban neighborhood in Florida in the hope of getting a few terrorists before they attack.

Let's be careful of guilt by association. Over the years, I've tried this on group after group, speaking a word and seeing what word comes immediately to mind. And a few words

First Sunday

down the line I say "Palestinian" and the immediate reaction is "terrorist." Most of the Palestinians I've known through the years are gentle, loving, sensitive, and in many cases well-educated persons -- not terrorists.

Let's never forget, God is a God of justice. Revenge is His, not ours. Jesus Christ is victor.

If we know, without doubt, who the perpetrators of these crimes are, we must bring them to the bar of justice and hold them accountable. But let us not inadvertently become, in vindictiveness and retribution, the very hate-filled evil that we so deplore.

Insight ten: Cast your cares on the Lord.

That's the bottom line, final statement. Psalm 55:22-23 reads: Cast your cares on the Lord and he will sustain you; he will never let the righteous fall. But you, O God, will bring down the wicked into the pit of corruption; bloodthirsty and deceitful men will not live out half their days. But as for me, I trust in you.

Do you believe that? Can you say that?

Remember, God loves you, and He loves every single person who has been impacted by this national tragedy. The clearest statement of what Christianity is all about is in those words of Jesus: For God so loved the world that he gave his one and only Son, that whoever believes in him shall not perish but have eternal life (John 3:16).

God created you with purpose and intentionality. God knows that something has gone wrong in your life and my life. God has taken the initiative to come in human form, to die on the cross for your sin and mine, through His resurrection to offer you and me forgiveness, meaning, and the strength to live in this world, equipping us to live in the life beyond this life in heaven with Him.

If you have never repented of sin and put your trust in Jesus Christ alone for salvation, do it today. Let this national tragedy be a wake-up call. Come to Jesus. Join the family of God called the church of Jesus Christ. Live for Him the rest of your life here, whether it be fifty years or twelve more hours, knowing He offers you eternity in heaven with Him if you'll put your faith in Him -- casting all your cares on Him.

First Sunday

Pastor Eun-sang Lee

*Warren United Methodist Church
Denver, CO*

Sunday, September 16, 2001

I wanted to connect with the people in the pew, give expression to what they might have been feeling and thinking, and create a space where we calm down and listen to the deeper voice of God. I did not want to offer an answer which I did not have. Rather, I wanted to be helpful to people, through sharing my own struggle, as they searched for their own responses to the event. This manuscript does not touch on the given gospel text, which was the lectionary gospel reading for that Sunday, but the image of God persistently searching for the lost ones became the source of inspiration. I mentioned that as part of gospel reading.

I don't remember anybody in the congregation who had a direct link to the event. Several people expressed to me their appreciation for my comment on needing to stand with our Muslim sisters and brothers. Violent reactivity against Arabs and the Islamic religion in general in my community was at a dangerous level as I believe was true in other parts of the nation.

Church attendance in the US spiked following 9-11 and within a year it came back to the "normal" level before the event. The conditions that led to the tragedy and the conditions that have dictated our responses since are still with us. And I'm still seeking: What do we uphold as people of God, as followers of Christ?

Voices Yet To Be Heard

Luke 15:1-10

Elie Wiesel said something like by simply talking about it we diminish the tragedy. I knew I would have to face you and talk about it. I dreaded that prospect. My heart sank heavy. Not just because of the memory of nightmares I used to have brought back by the tragic scene on the TV screen, the nightmares sown in me, the stories of civilians killed by indiscreet bombings and people buried alive by the forces on both sides of the Korean war. What is there for me to talk about? Plenty of words already, maybe too many of them, of the experts on terrorism and geopolitics and child psychology - I'm none of that. Words of religious leaders and preachers, too, and I am one, also, but whenever I try to forge my thoughts and feelings in words, I begin to well up, rather than speak, I yearn for a voice, I yearn to hear, there will be peace, on earth, but I don't hear that, it seems so distant. Words of military retribution, not just words but the inevitably imminent reality of it, and the consequent spiral of violence become fear in me. I know, in my heart, I'm a pacifist. I belong to those 7 per cent of

First Sunday

Americans who desire no military action at all. Probably I'm not the right kind of person to talk about this.

I understand why there will be military action. I'm grateful that people in the responsible position distinguish justice from revenge, at least in words.

And I believe, and pray, that the leaders of our nation will use our military forces responsibly. The burden of restrained use of force falls on the side of the more powerful. But, deep in my heart, I believe peace, the kind of peace Isaiah talked about, Jesus talked about, the lasting peace that has been the elusive collective yearning of the human race, won't be obtained through war making.

I feel tremendous anger at such a disrespect of human life. I have tremendous fear of what is to unfold. Mostly, I feel sorrow. Deep, deep sadness.

At the innocent lives lost, at the agony of their loved ones, at the kind of world we live in, at the kind of human evil our children have to be exposed to, at the predictable reaction of the religious right, and at demonizing of the whole group of people, religion and culture. Immediately, and very predictably, Arab-Americans and students from the Middle East were targeted at the time they most needed our embrace. Mosques had to be shut down when the Muslim community most needed them. The president of an Islamic school in New York City said she had to shut down the school because of the threat on the lives of children. "If that is the way it is to be," she said in perfect English, with New York accent at that, "I believe the terrorists have already won."

Don't let our children learn that they are not accepted, even hated, because of the difference, because of who they are.

Don't let them learn to see the world as us and them. The scars on their psyche will come back to society. There will be a cost to all of us.

Probably most disturbing to many Americans would be the picture of people jumping up and down with exhilaration on the streets of Palestine, many of them children.

In some sense, that scene is as predictable as the anti-Arab sentiment by some here in this country. With carefulness, I want to say two things about that. One is, as hard it might be for us, we have to try, very hard, to understand the deep-seeded sense of oppression, injustice and powerlessness of many Palestinians. Two, I don't believe, for a second, that is the whole picture.

However sensational that picture might be to the media operators, there must be, I believe, many people in that part of the global village who are as shocked and terrified and saddened as we are, who yearn for peace as we do.

First Sunday

Once, a professor at my college in South Korea told us the story of his visit to a sister university in Japan. Before and during the World War II Korea had been occupied by Japan. It had been truly brutal. During his visit, the professor said, a group of Japanese professors took him to a small basement room. And they told him, every morning all through the war, they would gather in that room to pray for the timely ending of the war, which would certainly have meant military defeat of their own country, and for peace.

I believe the voices are there, not on TV, but somewhere out there, and we have to hear them heart to heart.

We all are going through this whirlwind of emotions. Not just us. Families and friends in South Korea called me on that very day. This horror in America, that's all they were watching on TV all day. In the Hebrew Scripture is the story of prophet Elijah. Once his life was threatened by King Ahab and his wife Jezebel. Elijah ran for his life, alone, through the desert and into a mountain cave. He wanted to die. Then God came to him there. First there was a great wind, splitting mountains and breaking rocks in pieces. Peculiar, Bible says God was not in the wind. Then a ground shaking earthquake. But God was not in the earthquake. Then a fire, but God was not in the fire. A sound of sheer silence. Then came the voice of God in "a still small voice,"

Donald Robert Elton & Aura Agudo Elton

"What are you doing here, Elijah?"

Many voices we have heard. External voices of experts and leaders, and internal voices of anger, confusion and fear. Whirlwind of words and emotions. And I yearn to hear that still small voice of God. The voice of true consolation, and peace, the lasting peace in my heart and among the nations. In times like this, what is the best we can offer to America and to the world as the people of God, as the followers of Jesus Christ, as the bearers of the message of the cross and the resurrection? What is the very essence of our religion which we will uphold with our feeble hands?

One voice I'll never forget is the voice of a fireman in the dark pile of rubble, a stream of light coming out from the flesh light he holds in his hand, into the darkness,

"Anybody there?"

First Sunday

Rabbi Ellen Lewis

The Jewish Center of Northwest Jersey
Washington, NJ

September 29, 2001

In the Jewish community, we always joke that the holidays come "early'" or "late" but never on time. That is because of the way the Hebrew calendar operates. The high holy days (Rosh Hashana followed ten days later by Yom Kippur) can come as early as the first week in September or as late as the very end of September into October.

9-11 occurred in a year when the high holy days were "late." Usually we rabbis like that because it gives us more time to craft our sermons for Rosh Hashana and Yom Kippur without sacrificing summer vacation time. In the case of 9-11, however, rabbis whose sermons were already written immediately questioned themselves: How can I give this sermon in the light of 9-11? Will I have to rewrite all my high holy day sermons to make them relevant to this moment? These questions were reflected online in our rabbinic list-serve. I remember that one of my colleagues finally brought an end to all this panic by asking simply, why change what you've written? If you have been preaching about the eternal themes of the high holy days (yamim nora'im, literally "days of awe"), you should have no reason to change what you have prepared. And if you haven't been preaching about those themes - self-reflection, sin and repentance, life and death, taking an accounting of your life and vowing to do better - why aren't you?

And so I felt comfortable using essentially what I had prepared and altering it only to reflect the immediate tragedy of 9-11.

After 9-11, all synagogues had been contacted by the state (New Jersey) and told to be on high security alert. In my small rural congregation, we had always dismissed the idea of needing substantial security since people claimed to have a hard time finding us even when they were looking for us. We had as usual asked the local police to have a squad car outside during our worship, but when we looked for them, we realized they had not shown up. We called and were told that every spare police officer had rushed to the World Trade Center site to see if they could help.

In New Jersey, the state immediately closed the major highways. Public transportation came to a standstill. Two members of the congregation who work in Manhattan had somehow managed to get back to NJ either that night or the next morning. Everyone knew someone who had died or had been there or was supposed to have been there at that fateful moment. A pall hung over the state for months afterwards. I was supposed to have been working in my Greenwich Village office that day but had stayed home to work on sermons. My office was within view of the World

First Sunday

Trade Center. For months and years afterwards, when I looked out the window, all I saw was smoke and cranes.

My younger son was starting his freshman year in college but was still home since school didn't begin until the end of September. All his friends had already gone to school. My older son was already on campus in California. We had long ago purchased our tickets to San Francisco. When the airports closed, we weren't sure how we were going to get him to school. All the cross-country buses and trains were completely booked. As it turned out, the airports were open again by the time we needed to go. I remember sighing with relief on the return flight, as if his being in California would somehow be safer for him.

Life has gone on, of course. The air is no longer gritty with loss and the cranes have completed their work, but my heart still aches when I think about it.

EREV ROSH HASHANAH 2001-5762 TRAGEDY

Last Tuesday morning, as I sat in my safe kitchen and watched the TV screen as the World Trade Center fell, an old Yiddish proverb jumped into my head: "Human beings plan, God laughs." God wasn't laughing; but I did feel that for a moment, the veil of denial had been lifted for us all. We plan as if there is going to be a tomorrow. We live each day as if our lives will go on forever. We function as if we had all the time in the world. And much of the time, we get lucky. Our plans unfold as we had wished. The check really is in the mail; the babysitter shows up; the newspaper gets delivered; the baby arrives on its due date. We teach our children to be safe; we say, hold my hand when you cross the street, make sure you look both ways, wear your seat belt, just say no to drugs. But as I prepared to leave my house last Tuesday to run up to the supermarket, I stood looking at my alarm system, and said to myself, "Why bother?" What protection does a house alarm offer in a world like ours? And then I remembered the example of my teacher Rabbi Jakob Petuchowski zichrono livracha (may his memory be a blessing) and how he would plan. Every year for umpteen years, he flew from Cincinnati, Ohio to Laredo, Texas to be the rabbi of the tiny Reform congregation for the high holidays. Every year at the end of the holidays, before leaving Laredo, he would announce his sermon topics for the next high holidays. I used to admire his planning and feel inadequate ever to emulate it. Besides, I used to rationalize, how do you know what topic will be relevant a year hence? But the truth is that Jakob's advance planning was always relevant because he preached about the universal themes of these penitential holidays. He preached about how to live in a world where human beings plan and God laughs. So it is especially in the wake of tragedy on these holidays, when we feel that so much is beyond our control that we remind ourselves that we do have a plan, a spiritual one that has sustained us throughout the ages.

First Sunday

The first part of our plan includes taking an accounting of our souls and repenting our sins. Why respond to the tragedy of life by turning inward? It would seem that a more understandable response to tragedy might be external hatred and outward revenge. Certainly those were the immediate feelings of many of us last week. And yet we are told to turn inward and investigate ourselves instead. Why not indulge in hatred and demand revenge? The late Rabbi Shlomo Carlebach had an answer to that question. He was a European-born folksinger who immigrated to this country from Vienna when he was a teenager to escape the Nazis. Some years ago, he returned to give concerts in Vienna and several other cities in Austria and Germany. While there, he met with Austrian and German non-Jews as well as with Jews. Someone asked why he did it: "Don't you hate them?" he was asked. His answer was: "If I had two souls, I would devote one to hating them. But since I only have one, I don't want to waste it hating." Rabbi Harold Kushner says he has always been uncomfortable with the verse from the 23rd psalm when it says "Thou preparest a table before me in the presence of mine enemies" – he says it sounds like getting even with your enemies is the goal. But he felt better when he heard how Reb Zalman Schachter [currently known as Rabbi Zalman Schachter-Shalomi] understood that verse:

> Once a year, Reb Schachter throws an imaginary dinner party to which, in his mind, he invites all the people he is angry with, everyone who has hurt him

or disappointed him in the past year. In the course of that imaginary dinner, he goes around the table and thanks each of his guests for what they have taught him. Some have taught him not to expect too much of people because most people will put their own needs and their own well being ahead of other peoples' needs. And he thanks them for that important lesson. His philosophy has become, "When a friend makes a mistake, the mistake is still a mistake and the friend is still a friend." Some of his guests have taught him lessons about himself, driving him to ask himself why he was so bothered by something they did. What is it about him, his needs, his vulnerabilities that made the encounter so upsetting to him? And is it something he would want to change about himself to make himself less vulnerable to being upset? When he has gone around the table, thanking everyone on his enemies list for the lessons they have taught him, he is amazed at how much better he feels, cleansed of all that anger and resentment, able to maintain pleasant relationships even with flawed unreliable friends and relatives. And he thanks God for preparing a table before him in the presence of his enemies. Reb Schacter doesn't let hatred destroy his soul; he uses it as an opportunity for looking within and bettering his life.

First Sunday

This leads us to the second part of our spiritual plan. You see, by looking within and taking an accounting of our souls, we see that we, too, have the potential for committing evil acts and causing tragedy. In his book about the Gulag Archipelago, Solzhenitzen wrote, "If only it were so simple: if only there were evil people somewhere insidiously committing evil deeds and it were necessary only to separate them from the rest of us and destroy them. But the line dividing good and evil cuts through the heart of every human being. And who is willing to destroy a piece of his own heart?" It is better to understand what human beings are capable of, what we are capable of. The songwriter Leonard Cohen once wrote a prose piece called "All there is to know about Adolph Eichman":

Eyes: Medium
Hair: Medium
Weight; Medium
Height: Medium
Distinguishing features: None
Number of fingers: Ten
Number of toes: Ten
Intelligence: Medium

"What did you expect," Cohen writes? "Talons? Oversize incisors? Green saliva? Madness?" (<u>Stranger Music, Selected Poems and Songs</u> (McClelland & Stewart ISBN 077102231). Cohen would maintain that Eichman seemed quite average, not particularly evil. Yet we know that Eichman gave in to the power of evil within him. Our plan tells us: Don't give in to evil. These holidays tell us: Love the good within yourself. Love your life. Live as if you are really alive; don't wait or you might not get the chance again. Rabbi Jack Riemer expressed this idea in a piece he called "The view from the grandstand":

> O God all these good seats in the grandstand. It's so comfortable to be a fan. Sitting here in the stadium, I play no ball, I fight no fights. Down on the field, they're making mistakes. I could easily advise a sounder, more successful strategy. Up here in the stands, it's easier to spot boners on the field. Up here, I'm safe; nobody can say I blunder or boggle or make a single error. But God, they can say that the reason I never make errors is that I don't go out on the field. I do wish I could be more content with this role of spectator. I wish that being an observer of the game would keep me satisfied. But I'm nagged by the thought that maybe I should be down there on the field, mixing it up with all I've got. Give me, O God, a spirit of adventure, a spirit of boldness, so strong that I will enter the lists against some of the injustices that I see. Give me such an impulse to support good causes that I will forget to be cautious. Grant me the willingness to invest whatever energy I have in deeds that will bring strength to the weak and help to the sorrowing. May

First Sunday

I have such warmth of heart that I will champion those who need help. "

This is all part of the plan: Taking an accounting of your soul leads to repentance and repentance leads to new choices. This plan requires you not just to feel differently and see things differently but also to act differently. If you have been sitting on the sidelines of life, putting your energy into helping the sorrowing demonstrates how repentance can transform your life. In a famous Midrash, Elijah the prophet is standing at the gates of Rome. All about him, people are in rags, sick and starving. Elijah is bandaging the lepers one by one. A person approaches him and asks, "Pardon me, but aren't you the Mashiach ben David, the Messiah, son of David?" "Why yes," answers Elijah. "Well," continues the person, "in a world so full of pain and suffering, so surely in need of redemption, what are you waiting for?" Elijah lifts a fresh roll of bandages and thrusts it toward the stranger: "Indeed, and what are you waiting for?" In the aftermath of the World Trade Center tragedy, people didn't wait. Some gave their own lives in an attempt to save others. Thousands of people donated blood. One of the most touching calls that I received was from Israel from my friend Varda. What a turn this was, I thought, to get a call from Tel Aviv asking if I was all right. I told her: Today Americans know better what it feels like to be an Israeli. Israelis live with this kind of fear and uncertainty every day. They understand from sad experience that the only way to respond is by behaving as a community of human beings. Our plan has a lot to teach the world about surviving tragedy. The answer lies in this Hasidic story of two people wandering alone and lost in the forest. "I am lost," said the first: "I am glad to find you. Can you tell me the right road?" The second replied, "I too am lost. I do not know the right road. But let us join hands and continue our journey together." When we are lost, we join hands.

Our plan challenges us to take a roll of bandages and wrap it around the world and even around God. Rabbi Arnold Turetsky tells the story of going to the hospital and sitting with a man from out of town whose wife was seriously ill. The man sat there day and night, next to her bed, with nothing to do and no one to talk to. Rabbi Turetsky felt for him and did what he could to give him some strength. The man said to him, "Rabbi, I am not a believer. I have not been inside a synagogue for many years." Rabbi Turetsky replied: "If you would like to come to services this year, we would be glad to have you. You wouldn't need a ticket. You can just tell the usher you are a guest of mine." The man said, "Look rabbi, whatever I have to ask of God I can ask right here." Rabbi Turetsky said: "That's true, but maybe God has something to ask of you." Because our plan is actually God's plan; and what God would ask of us is simple: to know that the road to God goes through us. To know, as Buber would say, that God is found in our relationships. To know, as Elie Wiesel says, that there is more than one path leading to God but that the surest goes

First Sunday

through joy and not through tears. Our plan, God's plan, reminds us that eternity is present in every moment and that is how we should approach our lives, not despite but because of the tragedy of life. William James reminds us most clearly of what we know but had forgotten: "Any spirituality of joy is a spirituality of tragedy."

We plan and God laughs, says the Yiddish proverb. There is another Yiddish proverb that relates to our plan:

"Heaven and hell can both be had in this world." We had forgotten that truth for a moment. We had lived like it wasn't so. We had forgotten that if you want to bring heaven to earth, you have to have a plan. After God had rejected Cain's sacrifice, God said to Cain: "Why are you so upset? And why is your face fallen? Isn't this the way things are: If you do good, you'll be elevated, and if you don't do what's good, sin crouches at the door waiting and eager to get you. But you, you can rule over it." That, too, is part of the plan: We can rule over it and have known that since the days of Adam and Eve in the Garden of Eden.

The Midrash speaks of Adam at the termination of the first Sabbath when the sun sank and darkness began to set in. Terrified, Adam thought, "Surely indeed the darkness shall bruise me." God inspired Adam with knowledge and made him find two stone flints. One was marked with the name afelah, which is darkness; upon the other was inscribed the name mavet, which is death. With inspired knowledge,

Adam struck the flints against each other. The friction produced a spark with which he lit a torch. It comforted him through the night, and in the morning Adam saw the rising of the sun. He then observed: "This is the way of the world. Out of darkness and death, a spark is created. There is darkness and there is light, the fear of death and the hope of survival."

First Sunday

Rev. Keith Linkous

New Covenant Pentecostal Holiness Church
Princeton, WV

Wednesday, September 13, 2001

I remember exactly where I was at when the attacks of 9-11 took place. My wife and I were on vacation in North Carolina. As we got on the tram at North Carolina Zoological Park in Asheboro, the driver said, "Did you hear about the plane hitting that building in New York." We had not. Then she said, "Yeah, it hit, like, the New York Stock Exchange or something." I thought it was tragic, but I never anticipated the other events that would unfold throughout that morning. Then someone later told us that another plane had hit another building in New York City and that a plane had also hit the Pentagon in Washington, D.C. It was then that I knew something major was taking place.

After some discussion, my wife and I decided to cut our vacation short and head back home. I was in touch with some of our leaders from the church, and I told them I was coming back early. I wanted to be there for our people… and for our community. Plus, we had no way of knowing what else might occur that day … or in the days ahead.

Donald Robert Elton & Aura Agudo Elton

President George Bush called for a National Day of Mourning on that Friday, and our church opened its doors to the community to come in and pray and spend time with God. It was a very sober and somber time, and several people came that did not go to our church…but they knew they wanted to draw close to God during this time.

As for me, I could not get the images of the planes…the panic…the pain…and the people out of my mind. When it came time to prepare for the Sunday service, I knew that this was an opportunity to speak something significant to our church, to the Body of Christ at large, and to any guests that may attend that day. We were all in shock, and we knew that the only way we could face this national tragedy is with God's help.

As I sat in my office that weekend, I knew I wanted to speak to three things: First, I wanted to comfort people in their grief. Secondly, I wanted to let people know that God was not responsible for what happened. And thirdly, I wanted to use this opportunity to remind us all of what was and is really important.

I am so very humbled by the opportunity to have those words, which were spoken on the heels of America's greatest tragedy, included in this book. Though I no longer serve as pastor at the church where I preached this sermon, I do pray that the message that I sought to

First Sunday

communicate then is also the message that is communicated now. And I pray that we will never forget…

Facing Terrorism Firsthand

On Tuesday Morning, September 11, 2001, the United States of America, this blessed land, was the recipient of the worst terrorist attack in the world's history, forever altering our way of thinking and our way of life. America will never, and should not ever, be the same. America has now been tragically and dramatically quickened to the reality of the cautious lifestyle that exists in nations such as Israel, who must take extreme measures to ensure the safety and security of their people.

What many, and perhaps, most Americans thought would never happen, now has. The impossible has now become reality. We were targeted, we were hit, and we have been hurt deeply. This grave infiltration of our security and safety has left a forever impression on the heart and soul of every citizen.

This diabolical attack on our country has left a bigger void than the one in the New York skyline. There are voids in businesses, in homes, in families, in marriages, and in countless lives. Marriage partners are now widows and widowers. Parental pride has turned into parental pain. Good friends have become grieving friends.

Donald Robert Elton & Aura Agudo Elton

And this nation, though it is still a superpower by all means, has now also become a support group for those in sorrow and pain, which is shared by all American citizens. Future plans have become funeral plans. Hope has become hurt, peace has become pain, and confidence has become confusion. And there is a void in our hearts - of understanding, of comprehension, and for many loved ones, whose lives were swept away in an extreme and unthinkable act of terrorist violence. America has been wounded.

Countless questions abound. The pain gives rise to perplexity, as we experience various emotional reactions to this horrific scene, which seems like a dream, but has, each and every moment, proved to be all too real.

This is no dream - this is a nightmare. A nightmare of reality from which some, without God's help, will never awake. They are prospective prisoners to perpetual grief, pain, bitterness, hurt, and anger. And for them we must pray - earnestly and intently - we must pray.

We must pray for the families of the victims, for their loss, and the horror they are continually experiencing. We must pray for the rescue and recovery workers, who have tirelessly worked to recover any and all persons, regardless of the condition in which they are found.

First Sunday

We must pray for the eyewitnesses, whose minds will replay over and over for them the images of terror they saw firsthand. We must pray for the families of those who perpetrated these crimes, knowing that pain is not prejudiced, and that it's possible that their hearts are hurting too.

We must pray for our national leaders, from the President, to the investigators who are working to find those responsible. Pray for God's wisdom to be theirs, as they seek to bring the culprits to justice. We must pray for our nation - that the unity which this tragedy has brought, would remain and would increase, and that all of those who now have their eyes turned God-ward, would stay focused upon Him, realizing Him to be the one and only hope to guide us through, both this time of crisis, and the times of calm.

No person can navigate their way through these stormy seas without the help of our Sovereign God. Let's pray, that those who are now reaching out in desperation will become disciplined and determined to make the practice of prayer and reaching out to God a daily decision in their lives.

And we must pray for one another. May this past week's events serve as a wake-up call to the Body of Christ, concerning that which is really important, issues that really matter. May we learn these lessons well, so we don't have to be taught again, for the cost of this course is way too expensive. May we learn the folly of denominational divisiveness, and the importance of Christian collectivity and unity, which is God's initial purpose and design.

And may we learn to live a life of love and forgiveness. Let us realize the utter futility of feuding and fighting, of grudges and gossip, and of preferences and prejudices. May we not be outdone by the people of this great nation, who have dropped racist, religious, and all other prejudices, for the common good of uniting in solidarity, in order to better survive this difficult time in our nation.

May we also remember, that the deceased - whether victims or the perpetrators of these horrible acts - have now reached their eternal destinies. May this serve as a sober reminder for all of us of the severity and serious nature of that one decision to serve Jesus Christ, and to do so wholeheartedly, and may it ignite a compassionate fire in each of us for world evangelization, in hopes of preparing as many as possible to escape an eternity in hell, and to enter into an eternity in heaven.

May the Church, Christ's people, set the pace in unity, forgiveness, and healing, asking God to help solve outstanding issues in the Church, so we can offer true consolation and instruction to all American people, which are directly, or indirectly connected to this tragedy.

First Sunday

May we see that we ourselves are securely surrendered to God, knowing that we will not truly help anyone through exhortation, but through example. They will heed our words, only if those words are matched by our walk. May they see in our lifestyle, in tracing the trail of our steps, that we are continuously before God, yielded to His sovereignty, His Spirit, and His Authority. And that we are daily practitioners of those things we now exhort them to do.

Our prayer and hope must be, that unity will prevail over division. That purpose will prevail over prejudice. That America will prevail over adversity. That triumph will prevail over tragedy. That hope will prevail over hurt, that blessing will prevail over bitterness, and that prayer will prevail over pain.

May this tragedy serve to ignite the realization of the need to unite - in America and in the Church - and may God be with us, guiding us, keeping us, directing our steps. Let us not let this act of cowardice keep us in any constraint, except to the purpose of prayer, righteousness, and total yielded-ness and submission to God.

May we learn to trust God even more, depending upon His strength, His Power, and His Word. May God rule and reign in every community in this country, and may we remember, that with God, both the Church and America, can rise above this, and come out the better, learning invaluable and indispensable lessons of life, love, and liberty.

May God grant us all grace, peace, and mercy to survive the days ahead. May God bless us each and every one, and may God Bless America!

First Sunday

Rev. Michael McCartney

New Life Community Church
Amery, WI

Saturday, September 15, 2001

When I wrote this sermon I was pastoring at New Life Community Church in Amery, Wisconsin. The day 9-11 happened I was in my classroom where I taught High School Special Education in Clayton, Wisconsin. I was a part-time teacher at the time as well as a full-time pastor. Someone came down the hall and was telling all of us to turn on our TV's in the room because something terrible had just happened. My students all huddled around the TV as we turned on the TV to see the smoke billowing from the tower's burning and leaving a trail of smoke. We watched in silence and disbelief as footage kept coming forth then the first tower collapsed and a few of my students shrieked in horror.

The scene that day over the school was dark and gloomy. After making small chat one of my students spoke up and said "Where is the hope for those people?" Another student spoke up and said "I am not afraid because they blew up a big city - I would be more afraid if a plane had hit a small town like ours." We talked about hope, courage, even God as they were asking why God did not stop this from happening.

Donald Robert Elton & Aura Agudo Elton

We talked about heroes, sorrows and terrorism that day. This day of tragedy, reflection and discussion with me and a bunch of high school students compelled me to write my sermon for that following Sunday. I prepared the message thinking of the comment "Where is the Hope?" I delivered that message to New Life and it was also aired on the local cable station as well. Many shared with me how they felt hope after hearing my message both in the service and on the air.

I had many conversations with unbelievers after this event about how we need to be ready at any moment to meet the Lord. One person in my church who was new to the area had just moved there from New York. She told me that every morning she walked through the base of the towers to get breakfast and coffee on her way to work. She knew many people who were impacted by the collapse. She was so thankful that they had decided to move to a small town and semi-retire. She is now a professional counselor at the local hospital today, helping others go through a healing process.

As I look back nine years I still know that there is help beyond terrorism and his name is Jesus. It comforts me even now to know all the stories that came out of that tragedy and How even in the midst of tragedy God is there to bring hope and healing.

First Sunday

Hope Beyond Terrorism

We have been shocked by terrorism like never before this week and many are walking around bewildered saying, "Where is the hope?"

Lets recap the Timeline of the week that has caused many to be bewildered and feeling hopeless: On September 11, a date that will live in infamy for Americans, terrorists attacked the World Trade Center in New York City. At 9:05 a.m., hijacked United Airlines Flight 175, carrying 65 people, crashes into the South tower. The North tower burns from a previous crash of American Airlines Flight 11 at 8:48 a.m.. "I was in the World Financial Center looking out the window," said one woman. "I saw the first plane, and then 15 minutes later saw the other plane just slam into the World Trade Center." Another woman said: "It was the most horrible thing I've ever seen in my life."

A person jumps from the North Tower of the World Trade Center as another clings to the outside, left center, while smoke and fire billow from the building. "About five minutes before the tower fell, you could see people jumping from the upper floors. I watched six either fall or jump...." said Steve Johnson, a MSNBC.com producer who was standing about six blocks from the towers in lower Manhattan.

At 9:59 a.m., the South Tower collapses. People in front of St. Patrick's Cathedral react as they look down Fifth Avenue toward the World Trade Center. "Clearly, not even the police and FBI who had flooded the area were worried about collapse, they wouldn't have been anywhere as near to the buildings as they were. If the first building hadn't essentially fallen straight down, its crash could have killed hundreds standing, like me, a few blocks away," said George Hackett of Newsweek.

At 10:28 a.m., the North Tower comes crashing down. Mike Smith, a fire marshal from Queens, said: "Everyone was screaming, crying, running — cops, people, firefighters, everyone. A couple of marshals just picked me up and dragged me down the street."

With the Washington Monument in the background, a hijacked American Airlines Flight 77 crashes into the Pentagon. "I'm totally freaked out. Hearing the plane going over my head was frightening," said Elissa Brainard, 29.

All domestic airports were shut down after four commercial airliners were hijacked and then crashed. Passengers leave under the watchful eye of a Massachusetts State trooper in the American Airlines terminal at Logan Airport in Boston.

First Sunday

Quotes from NBC news at NBCnews.com.

Yes, we have been faced with one of the worst weeks in the history of this nation. We have about 260 people killed on the high jacked airplanes. 190 people killed at the Pentagon. 184 confirmed dead at the World Trade center with 4,763 people missing and presumed dead. The death total of the World Trade Center, the Pentagon, the 4 air planes brings the death toll to over 5,000 individuals who lost their lives this week. Compare that to Pearl Harbor 2,390 and the Titanic 1,500 the combination of these two tragedies still does not match what happened this week in total loss of life. Yet you need to understand these were people just like you and me. They had parents, brothers, sisters, spouses, friends, and children.

Where is the Hope! All these lives gone in a moment of time! Unexpected devastation in a moment in time! Men and women like you and me just going through their daily routine come face to face with terrorism and its death and destruction. But I want to tell you, "There is hope for the present and the future!" Many would reply that yes its in the Military, or its in more Intelligence, or its in our vast wealth, or it's in patriotism. A president of the United States once talked about where true hope comes from:

In June of 1863, just weeks before the battle of Gettysburg, a college President asked Lincoln if he thought the country would survive. President Lincoln replied: I do not doubt that our country will finally come through safe and undivided. But do not misunderstand me… I do not rely on the patriotism of our people …the bravery and devotion of the boys in blue…(or) the loyalty and skill of generals… But the God of our fathers, Who raised up this country to be the refuge and asylum of the oppressed and downtrodden of all nations, will not let perish now. I may not live to see it … I do not expect to see it, but God will bring us through safe.

This is a key my brothers and sisters in Christ. Our hope comes from the Gospel, from the Lord Jesus Christ!

We have learned this week that we are not in control and this has shattered many people's hope?

The 12 Step program of recovery starts out telling us we need to admit we are powerless over our situation-that our lives have become unmanageable.

America recognized for the first time how helpless – how we are not in control of everything around us. One teacher in a school told his students that he had been been wrong when he had told them earlier that a terrorist attack could never happen in America. He admitted that he was wrong. It can happen in America! I heard of Senators saying this cannot be true, "Not in The United States!" But they realized it was not a movie it was reality-it happened and it can happen again! We are not in control like we think we

First Sunday

are. To recognize this is the first step to healing our nation - our lives! Listen to me God is in control not you, not me - not others!

Romans 7:17, which speaks directly to this life predicament, "I know nothing good lives in me, that is in my sinful nature. For I have the desire to do what is good, but I cannot carry it out." Man's nature without the Lord is evil-there is no good in man without the spirit of God!

Step two speaks to us about our brokenness and inability to fix ourselves. Step two centers us in on a "Higher Power" this higher power is the Lord Jesus Christ. He is the one with the power to restore my life and repair my broken condition. Only God can heal this nation! Only God can restore and rebuild it. The foundation of humanism is destroying our country.

This week at a school in the area the student made a flag out of imprints of their hand and wrote God Bless America over the flag. One teacher commented to another teacher – This is crossing the line of separation of Church and State! The biggest lie being promoted today in our country.

What? This person does not want God to bless our nation in a tragic time?

What? This person does not want God to bless our schools?

What? This person does not want God to bless the hurting?

No nation survives without God - Ask the Soviet Union. If this person does not want God to bless our nation or our schools then maybe this person should move to a communist country! There where other teachers who did not do the moment of silence in some schools – this attitude is what is wrong with our nation today and what is making this nation vulnerable to terrorists attacks.

II Chronicles 7:14,15a

14 if my people, who are called by my name, will humble themselves and pray and seek my face and turn from their wicked ways, then will I hear from heaven and will forgive their sin and will heal their land. 15 Now my eyes will be open and my ears attentive to the prayers...

I have to come to the conclusion here, that I cannot repair myself. Christ is the one who is able to put me back together. Christ is the one who can repair the hurt, the devastation of this nations recent tragedies.

This scenario reminds me of the Old Nursery Rhyme, "Humpty Dumpty." Read it.

First Sunday

Let's make the rhyme more personal!

>Humpty Dumpty sat on a wall.
>(Doing his daily routine.)

>Humpty Dumpty had a great fall;

>(because the wall was blown up by terrorists.)

>All the Kings horses, and
>all the kings men
>Cannot put Humpty Dumpty
>together again.

>(All the world's ways and my ways cannot put this nation back together again.)

But when the natural ways, and my ways fail, I'm promised through the Words of Christ that He can put me back together again if I place my faith in Him. The Lord is speaking to this nation from Phil. 2:12 "God is working in you to make you willing and able to obey Him."

This progresses us to step 3 which involves the decision to let God be in charge of our lives the ONLY HIGHER POWER!

Donald Robert Elton & Aura Agudo Elton

Romans 12:1, 2 speaks to us here

"Dear Friends, God is good. So I beg you to offer your bodies to Him as a living sacrifice, pure and pleasing. That's the most sensible way to serve God. Don't be like the people of this world, but let God change the way you think. Then you will know how to do everything that is good and pleasing to Him." (CEV) But we must make this decision to turn our will to God! Through our brokenness, pain, disappointments and our suffering, there is a promise to all those who suffer. Jesus said, "Come to me, all you who are weary and burdened and I will give you rest, take my yoke upon you and learn from me, for I am gentle and humble of heart, and you will find rest for your souls. For my yoke is easy and my burden is light." (Matt. 11:28-30)

The invitation is still for us today. But the decision is up to each one of you to accept it! It's up to this nation to drop to their knees and turn their lives toward God rather than turn their backs on the Lord!

If you accept His invitation you will receive Hope! Strength! and Peace!

From Preaching Today - The movie Amistad is about a slave ship filled with abducted African men, women, and children. In the face of starvation, beatings, rape, and murder, the Africans plan a coup on route from Africa to

First Sunday

Cuba. On a stormy night, their leader, Cinque, unshackles his comrades. They seize the ship and order the planter to sail them to Africa. Instead of navigating them to Africa, however, the planter lands them to an eastern American seaport, where the Africans are imprisoned. On the eve of the judge's verdict, the Africans are scattered about their prison cell, lost in their despondency. But one sits contentedly in a corner reading a Bible given by a missionary. Cinque, the fearless leader, glumly looks over at his fellow captive, Yamba, and says, "You don't have to pretend to be interested in that. Nobody's watching but me."

Lets pick it up there!

The closing scene: gazing intently at Cinque, Yamba insists, "This is where the soul goes when you die here. This is where we're going when they kill us." Stroking the picture that depicts heaven, Yamba concludes, "It doesn't look so bad."

T.S. - When you accept the one who really gives hope and healing then you get to see what Hope we have in Christ Jesus. Revelation gives us just a little glimpse:

The Holy Bible, New International Version

Revelation 21:1 (NIV)

1 Then I saw a new heaven and a new earth, for the first heaven and the first earth had passed away, and there was no longer any sea.
2 I saw the Holy City, the new Jerusalem, coming down out of heaven from God, prepared as a bride beautifully dressed for her husband.
3 And I heard a loud voice from the throne saying, "Now the dwelling of God is with men, and he will live with them. They will be his people, and God himself will be with them and be their God.
4 He will wipe every tear from their eyes. There will be no more death or mourning or crying or pain, for the old order of things has passed away."
5 He who was seated on the throne said, "I am making everything new!" Then he said, "Write this down, for these words are trustworthy and true."
6 He said to me: "It is done. I am the Alpha and the Omega, the Beginning and the End. To him who is thirsty I will give to drink without cost from the spring of the water of life.
7 He who overcomes will inherit all this, and I will be his God and he will be my son.
8 But the cowardly, the unbelieving, the vile, the murderers, the sexually immoral, those who practice magic arts, the idolaters and all liars—their place will be in the fiery lake of burning sulfur. This is the second death."

Revelation 21

First Sunday

EVERYTHING NEW

I saw Heaven and earth new-created. Gone the first Heaven, gone the first earth, gone the sea.
I saw Holy Jerusalem, new-created, descending resplendent out of Heaven, as ready for God as a bride for her husband.

I heard a voice thunder from the Throne: "Look! Look! God has moved into the neighborhood, making his home with men and women! They're his people, he's their God. He'll wipe every tear from their eyes. Death is gone for good—tears gone, crying gone, pain gone—all the first order of things gone." The Enthroned continued, "Look! I'm making everything new. Write it all down—each word dependable and accurate."

Then he said, "It's happened. I'm A to Z. I'm the Beginning, I'm the Conclusion. From Water-of-Life Well I give freely to the thirsty. Conquerors inherit all this. I'll be God to them, they'll be sons and daughters to me. But for the rest—the reckless and faithless, degenerates and murderers, sex peddlers and sorcerers, idolaters and all liars—for them it's Lake Fire and Brimstone. Second death!"
16. Never again will they hunger; never again will they thirst. The sun will not beat upon them, nor any scorching heat. 17. For the Lamb at the center of the throne will be

their shepherd; he will lead them to springs of living water. And God will wipe away every tear from their eyes."

Rev. 21:23,24 "The city does not need the sun or the moon to shine on it, for the glory of God gives it light, and the lamb is its lamp. The nations will walk by its light, and the kings on the earth will bring their splendor into it."

Rev. 22:4,5 " They will see His face, and His name will be on their foreheads. There will be no more night. They will not need the light of a lamp or the light of the sun, for the Lord God will give them light. And they will reign for ever and ever."

Those who perished in the attacks that knew Jesus Christ are now in the presence of God dwelling with him in His city where there are no more tears, no more pain but a place filled with joy and love. Scripture also tells us in revelations other things about this Holy City. In Revelation 21 and 22 we learn about the residents of the Holy City. Revelation 21; 10 states, "And in the spirit he carried me away to a great, high mountain and showed me the holy city Jerusalem coming down out of heaven from God." Moore makes this observation that I would like to expand on today, "In the verses that follow (Revelation 21 and 22), John describes the unique characteristics of that holy city. Now, the promise of Revelation is that, if you're a believer (i.e. in the language of Revelation, you have had your "robe washed in the blood of the Lamb"), you will

First Sunday

someday inhabit that holy heavenly city in the New Heaven!" If you know Jesus!

T.S.- Lets take a few moments today and explore this Holy city and learn what it is like and what those who perished that knew Christ are having the pleasure of partaking of.

God's Glow in the Holy City – I believe MANY who perished are saying right now WOW what a show! Revelation 21, 22 - Gives us a glimpse of what happens when God shows up and glows in a city. The Holy city's first characteristic is God dwells in it (21:3). God – Yes – Dwells, resides, lives, in this city LITERALLY! In this city crying is done away with as God wipes away all the pain and sorrow and hurt. (21:4) Those who knew Jesus do not have to experience this. In other words there is joy, happiness, contentment! That is what he is enjoying right now. In this city there is No death – only life - life with no crying, no pain. Death is no longer a concern only life! What is a city like when God glows and sits on the throne in a city? There is no death, no pain, no sorrow! Those who perished will never have to experience anymore pain.

In this holy city there is a new way of doing things – the old is dead and gone – It means: This city is not like the worlds - driven by pride, by greed, by people treading on top of others to get to the top, by people doing their own thing at the cost of someone else's life or feelings. No this city is run with Love in absolute control. (21:4-10).

Reflect on I Cor. 13 "The Love chapter!"
NIV 1 Corinthians 13:4-13

4. Love is patient, love is kind. It does not envy, it does not boast, it is not proud.

5. It is not rude, it is not self-seeking, it is not easily angered, it keeps no record of wrongs.

6. Love does not delight in evil but rejoices with the truth.

7. It always protects, always trusts, always hopes, always perseveres.

8. Love never fails. But where there are prophecies, they will cease; where there are tongues, they will be stilled; where there is knowledge, it will pass away.

9. For we know in part and we prophesy in part,

10. But when perfection comes, the imperfect disappears.

11. When I was a child, I talked like a child, I thought like a child, I reasoned like a child. When I became a man, I put childish ways behind me.

12. Now we see but a poor reflection as in a mirror; then we shall see face to face. Now I know in part; then I shall know fully, even as I am fully known.

13. And now these three remain: faith, hope and love. But the greatest of these is love.

First Sunday

In this city God makes everything new - there are no ghettos, no crack houses, no houses of ill repute, no exploitation of people and resources, no thieves stealing – no it's ALL NEW! It's all fresh and beautiful! There is a new government!

In this city there is a spring of everlasting life. Many have looked for the fountain of youth so they could live forever. Here it is friends it's in the New Jerusalem (21:6). The great blessing is, there is no cost to drink of its life giving water. Those who knew Christ in the attacks have discovered the fountain of life. In this city according to Rev. 21:11 "It shone with the Glory of God, and its brilliance was like that of a precious jewel, like jasper, clear as crystal." Friend the holy city was illuminated with the presence of God. There was a beautiful colorful majestic view of GOD! It is absolutely breath taking. PAUSE AND LET HIS SPIRIT GIVE YOU A GLIMPSE!!!!

Remember some who perished are experiencing this right now! The walls and foundations glittered and beam with the brilliant colors of beauty. The gates are white washed pearls. The streets are paved in GOLD (21:11-21)! WOW what a show.

This city had no temple – no church buildings - because God along with the lamb resided there literally. You could see them, touch them, speak to them, hear them, and smell their sweet presence (21:22,23) Some who perished are right now enjoying the presence of God. 21:23 states, "The city does not need the sun or the moon to shine on it, for the glory of God gives it light, and the Lamb its lamp." In the city - God flows and glows and all can see the light. In this city a resident is one who has a personal relationship with the Lord God almighty. It's personal and intimate! It's not philosophical its real! I discover that a resident of this city walks in the light because of God's presence – they see by God's illuminating presence. There is no need of natural light because God's supernatural light is everywhere guiding the way around in the city. Jesus told us in John 8:12 "I am the light of the world. Whoever follows me will never walk in darkness, but will have the light of life." John tells us in I John 1:5 "…God is light in Him there is no darkness…" The Psalmist wrote of the Lord (Psalms 119:105) "Your word is a lamp to my feet and a light for my path." In this city we are told in verses 24-26 that the kings will honor and praise the Lord. Yes even the leaders and the whole nation will proclaim the Lord the king and bring him glory.

In this city everyone even the President and Congress type people will honor God. There will be no separation of Church and State. They are one because you cannot have good government without the Lord Almighty. The city will never close its gates again. All will be able to enter into the presence of the Lord. There will be no night. In Other

First Sunday

words night represents evil it will be banished forever! There will only be LIGHT! In this city the residents will worship God alone. They will not worship themselves only HIM! In the Holy City the residents will be holy and righteous. There will be no evil or unclean individuals. There will be no deception only truth. It will be full of residents who are written in the Lambs book of life. There will be no disgusting practices. No child abusers, no rapists, no violence, no crime, no murderers, no liars, no self-centered individuals, there will be only people who are blessings to each other.

In this city there will be mass production of great fruit. The resident there will receive fruit from the tree of life that will bring healing to everyone. The pains of the past will be completely healed. The diseases and sickness of life will be gone (Rev.22:1, 2). The residents of this city will receive fresh fruit all the time! They will be satisfied like never before! The fruit of Spirit will be manifested in the lives of the residents: Galatians 5:22-23 "The fruit of the Spirit is love, joy, peace, patience, kindness, generosity, faithfulness, and self-control."

In this city there will be no curses only blessings as God's people worship and Praise the Lord. The residents of this city will serve the Lord (Rev. 22:3,4). Because the curse is gone once again we will see his face like Adam and Eve. No more separation because of the curse. We will be united with Lord forever! In the city of Light where God's glows-flows - and shows we will reign with Him forever and ever.

Conclusion: We have been illuminated this mornings by the Holy Spirit and God's Word. Where is our hope? Swindoll states, "Hope is a wonderful gift from God, a source of strength and courage in the face of life's harshest trials:

When we are trapped in a tunnel of debris and blackness, hope points to the light at the end of the tunnel.

When our nation is rocked by hijackings, hope tells us to drop to our knees in prayer for renewal.

When we are overworked and exhausted from moving rubble away, hope gives us fresh energy.

When we are dismayed because of explosions, hope lifts our spirits.

When we are tempted to give up and surrender, hope says to push on.

When we are lost and confused from all the devastation, hope dulls the edge of panic.

First Sunday

When we struggle with over 5,000 people being killed by terrorists, hope brings reminders that God is still in control. When we fear that the worst is not over, hope reminds us our security is in Christ.

When we must endure the tragedy of bad choices, hope fuels our recovery.

When we find ourselves out of a job because our building has been blown up, hope tells us we still have a future because of Christ.

When we feel deserted and abandoned, hope reminds us we're not alone…we will make it with Christ.

When we say our final farewell to those who perished knowing Christ, hope in the life beyond gets us through our grief.

When life experiences hijackings, and planes driven into buildings and cries of pain and anguish, when dreams are crushed, when life hurts so much my soul aches, nothing helps like hope - hope in Christ!

Donald Robert Elton & Aura Agudo Elton

Pastor Travis Moore
Outreach Inc.
Vista, CA

June 24, 2002

Where Was God On 9-11-01?

"My God, my God, why have you forsaken me?"
(Mat 27:46)

Some events in human history impact us so greatly, that we will forever remember the circumstance surrounding where we were when we heard the news. I'll never forget sitting in a classroom while in the 8th grade and hearing the reports of JFK's assassination over the school PA system. Or watching with a group of teachers, students and school administrators as Christa McAuliffe began her journey to be the first teacher in space, only to have it end so abruptly and tragically. Nor will I ever forget stepping out of the shower at about 6:00 AM {CA time) to see smoke billowing up from the North Tower of the World Trade Center and moments later see the second plane crash into the South Tower. Those images are forever embedded in my memory. You no doubt remember exactly where you were and what you were doing when you first heard the news.

First Sunday

But today, I want to ask and attempt to answer the question that no doubt has puzzled so many since that horrific day:

Where was God on 9-11?

1. The same place He was when Adam rebelled in Eden – waiting to cover his sin. (Gen 3)
From the very beginning of human history man has acted in rebellion against God who made and loved him.

Creating man in His on image,
placing him in a perfect environment,
making him master over all creation,
providing for his every need, and
spending time with him in the beautiful garden...

were ways God demonstrated his love for the crown of His creation. But, albeit deceived by the evil one, man made a conscious decision to rebel against His Creator and Friend. Where was God when man first raised his ugly head of defiance and rebellion? Couldn't He have stopped it before it began? Oh, it is not a matter of whether or not He could have. It is a matter of His design for humanity and His plan of redemption. He designed us with a freedom of choice. In His sovereign foreknowledge He made provision before the world was ever created for man's redemption; knowing full well that man would make disastrous choices from the beginning. When Adam and Eve finally "fessed-up, He was there with a covering for their nakedness and shame;

exacting the ultimate punishment on an innocent victim to cover man's sin. But, He was there!

Where was God on 9-11?

2. The same place He was when Noah built an ark – protecting him from disaster. (Gen 6-9)

Sadly, man's rebellion did not end with Adam and Eve. Their sons, and their son's sons for every generation followed in their rebellious path. Until such time that the wickedness of man filled the whole earth and its stench rose as an offense to the Holiness of God. Yet in the midst of such ungodliness, "Noah found grace in the eyes of the Lord" (Gen 6:8). Here was a man, not a perfect, but a righteous man, who faithfully proclaimed the righteousness of God. (2 Pet 2) And when God, grieved by man's wicked rebellion, determined to wipe man from the face of the earth, He furthermore determined to spare Noah and his family, and from their stock repopulate planet earth. So in mankind's greatest natural disaster, God was on His throne protecting His own.

Where was God on 9-11?

3. The same place He was when Job lost everything he had {except a nagging wife} – proving Himself to be God despite unfortunate circumstances. (Job 1-2)

First Sunday

Just as Noah's generation experienced earth's greatest natural disaster, Job would surely rank among the top in man's history as experiencing the greatest personal disaster. Again we see a man, a good man, a godly man standing for what is right and hating what is wrong. Did being "blameless and upright" immune Job from problems, of even disaster? Of course not! Job lived on a planet that at times experienced natural disasters such as tornados, earthquakes and fire. There were evil men in his day, too, who were willing to kill and steal to get what they wanted. And, he became the special target of satanic fury. As a result, Job lost everything of value; even his precious children. Where was God? Had He turned His back on Job? Would Job return the favor by turning his back on God? No! No! and NO! God had not deserted Job. And Job would not curse God, even though he was urged to do so by a less than faithful wife.

Where was God when Job was losing all? Where was He when Job's children were killed? Where was He when Job's flesh was wracked with pain? Job maintained his integrity and recognized that it was God's prerogative to give and take, and it was his duty to "Bless the name of the Lord."

Where was God on 9-11?

4. The same place He was when Abraham lapsed in faith – safeguarding the fulfillment of His promise. (Gen 12-15) It might be successfully argued that today's struggles with radical Islamic fundamentalism are traceable to this unfortunate incident in Abraham's life. Abraham, the father of the faithful, had left his homeland at the prompting of his God and gone to a land that was to be given to his descendants after him. There was a slight problem, though. He had no descendants. He had a beautiful wife, lots of servants, and many possessions, but no descendants. How would God fulfill his promise? How could He? Abraham was already an old man. Sarah was well past the years of child bearing. Did God need a bit of help? Along comes Hagar. She was young, and her womb fertile. It was not uncommon in his day to find a surrogate mother to bear a child for a barren wife. Maybe God did need some help. There's nothing wrong with helping God out, is there? God does His part, and we have to do ours. So, to Abraham and Hagar is born a son, Ishmael, father of the modern Arab states. Not the son of promise. That distinction was to be reserved for Isaac, whom Sarah would eventually bear to Abraham when he was 100 years and she was 90.

First Sunday

Where was God on 9-11?

5. The same place He was when Joseph was rotting in jail – accomplishing His perfect will. (Gen 37-50)

If ever anyone was misunderstood and ill treated, it was Joseph. If ever anyone suffered wrongly, it was Joseph. Yet with all his hardships, problems and abuse, Joseph was able to honestly say, "You meant it for harm, but God meant it for good." This was certainly true in the case of his brothers selling him into slavery, Mrs. Potiphar falsely accusing him of attempted rape, and the lapse of memory of his Butler friend. Yet each step of the way, God was able to take Joseph's trying circumstance and mold him ever more closely into the man he would one day become. He was there all the time, though I am sure Joseph must have wondered at times.

Where was God on 9-11? We could go on and on and tell of experiences such as

6. ... Moses (Ex. 1-4) on the backside of the desert – being prepared for greater service.

7. ... Samson (Jud 14-16) groping in darkness – being strengthened in his hour of weakness.

8. ... Jonah (Johan 1-4) being swallowed by a fish – learning that God's way is best.

9. … Daniel (Dan. 6) being thrown to hungry lions – resting comfortably on a "lion-skin-rug" while jealous men sought to end his life because of his faithful testimony.

10. … Peter & John (Acts 3-5) beaten for preaching the Gospel – being given greater opportunities for sharing the good news of Christ.

11. … or Paul (Acts 14-28) being stoned, shipwrecked and imprisoned – yet being assured that all things work together for good to them who love God.

But maybe the greatest insight into the heart of God when a tragedy strikes such as the 9-11 Disaster is to respond …

Where was God on 9-11?

12. The same place He was when Jesus hung on the Cross – enduring the pain for the benefit of others. (Matt 27)

Oh the horror! Oh the agony! Oh the anguish! Oh the pain! Not just the thorns on His brow. Not just the lashes on His back. Not just the bruises from the reeds and fist of his captors. Not just he plucking of the beard from His face. Not just the spittle being hurled at Him. Not just the nails in His hands and feet. Not just the spear piercing His side. All this, yes; plus the weight of the sins of the world

First Sunday

pressing down on His shoulders.

Where was God when His one and only Son hung dying on the cross? Didn't He know? Couldn't He have prevented it; or stopped it? Was He helpless? Was He not aware? Didn't He care?

Of course He knew! Of course He could have prevented it! Of course He could have stopped it! Of course He wasn't helpless! Of course He was aware! And, Of course He cared! God knew it was happening, could have stopped it, ... but He didn't. Is He some kind of fiend? Of course not!

He had a larger picture in view. There was a greater good to be accomplished by the suffering and death of Jesus. Through the suffering of One, many would be made whole. Through the sacrifice of One, many would have their sins forgiven. Through the death of One, many would be made alive.

He wasn't just sitting idle and helpless as His Son suffered. He was using the schemes of wicked hearts to bring about the redemption of mankind. He reminds us that ... "my thoughts are not your thoughts, neither are your ways my ways," declares the Lord. "As the heavens are higher than the earth, so are my ways higher than your ways and my thoughts than your thoughts." (Isa 55:8-9)

Donald Robert Elton & Aura Agudo Elton

So we ask again …

Where was God on 9-11?

The Bottom Line:

God was not surprised by 9-11,
But He was saddened by it.
God did not cause 9-11,
But He does comfort those affected by it.
God may not prevent future acts of terrorism,
But He will provide peace to those whose hearts are filled with hatred if they will turn to Him.

First Sunday

Pastor Glenn Newton

New Hope Church of the Nazarene
Clarksville, Arkansas

Sunday, September 16, 2001

I remember thinking to myself that I couldn't allow my own anger to filter into what I was going to write. I spent a lot of time in prayer asking the Lord to show me what I needed to share with the church, what was the truth that they needed to hear, to take away from this tragedy. I pray of course over every message, but I remember spending many more hours just trying to listen to what God would have me say, because I knew it would be important to get it right.

As with any sermon, what I hoped to accomplish was to allow God to use me to preach His Word, His truth and to give the Church Hope.

We had a larger than normal crowd, that was the main difference I saw right away. We didn't have anyone who was personally involved in any way. It's hard to say how the congregation was influenced, especially this many years later, but I remember wanting to give them the truth that this was an act of evil, carried out by 13 men, but this evil is something that we will continue to battle with God's strength. I guess I was trying to remind them of the bigger picture, the spiritual battle that rages everyday.

9-11 was a wake up call for our nation in many ways, including spiritually. But, unfortunately, when the immediate threat seems to be gone, we go back to what we are comfortable doing. I believe we are more aware of what is going on around our world now. Our church has begun teaching about the "Christian" world view versus the other world views that are out there and how these ideas are in constant conflict. I know our church seems more in tune with what is going on in our national politics and policies that affect national security. I'm afraid we will endure another attack at some point. It seems like when you have this many enemies trying to harm you, enemies that are patient and working together, it will be hard to stop.

STAND FIRM

Ephesians 6:10
Finally, be strong in the Lord and in his mighty power. 11 Put on the full armor of God so that you can take your stand against the devil's schemes. 12 For our struggle is not against flesh and blood, but against the rulers, against the authorities, against the powers of this dark world and against the spiritual forces of evil in the heavenly realms. 13 Therefore put on the full armor of God, so that when the day of evil comes, you may be able to stand your ground, and after you have done everything, to stand. 14 Stand firm then, with the belt of truth buckled around your waist, with the breastplate of righteousness in place, 15

First Sunday

and with your feet fitted with the readiness that comes from the gospel of peace. 16 In addition to all this, take up the shield of faith, with which you can extinguish all the flaming arrows of the evil one. 17 Take the helmet of salvation and the sword of the Spirit, which is the word of God. 18 And pray in the Spirit on all occasions with all kinds of prayers and requests. With this in mind, be alert and always keep on praying for all the saints.

On Tuesday, September 11, 2001, we were invaded by the worst kind of enemy imaginable. We were invaded, our security was shattered, our sense of well being was pulled away as we watched in horror two great buildings and our Center of Defense, the Pentagon burn and crumble with thousands of lives lost.

We were invaded. Our comfortable lives, our own plans, our personal agendas were invaded by National pain, a loss of life that we have only experienced once before in one day, and that was during the Civil War. Never before had America lost so many lives in one day. We were invaded. This invasion was an invasion of evil, evil bent on destroying our Peace, Our Faith, Our Love. This invasion will not prevail. This Invasion of evil will be the day America Woke up from it's Spiritual Sleep.

Make no mistake this morning. This horrible invasion has so shook us as a Nation that We have been driven to our knees in Prayer. I Praise God for a President that has led our Nation to this time of Prayer, it was by his proclamation that Yesterday at noon was a National Call to Prayer.

Let me read a portion of President Bush's message he gave yesterday during this Prayer service,

"God's signs are not always the ones we look for. We learn in tragedy that his purposes are not always our own, yet the prayers of private suffering, whether in our homes or in this great cathedral are known and heard and understood. There are prayers that help us last through the day or endure the night. There are prayers of friends and strangers that give us strength for the journey, and there are prayers that yield our will to a will greater than our own."

We need to Thank God for a Leader that is looking to God during these times of Trial, and we need to Pray for all our leaders as very important decisions will be made in the coming days as we send our Men and Women into battle.

As I watched that Prayer Service where Rev. Billy Graham was the keynote speaker, I couldn't help but believe God has kept Billy Graham with us for this moment to help lead our Nation back to God. Listen to What God has promised, "14 if my people, who are called by my name, will humble themselves and pray and seek my face and turn from their wicked ways, then will I hear from heaven and will forgive

First Sunday

their sin and will heal their land." 2 Chronicles. 7:14

On Tuesday we were invaded by the worst kind of evil, on Saturday, we responded as a Nation, with all our leaders, in church, Seeking His Face, and asking for His guidance.

The question remains, will we repent of our sins as a Nation?

But I am excited about what God will do through this tragedy, we are at a time where more people are turning to God and to the Christian Faith for answers than anytime in my lifetime, and maybe yours too.

We were invaded by Evil, Cowards who were used as instruments in the hands of Satan. The question is How Will We Respond? This morning I'm asking this to you personally. We know how we will respond as a Nation, we are going to War, And we will do whatever it takes to win that War, because that's what Americans Do, We will Fight For Freedom and Justice until the battle is ours.

I have no doubt after watching and hearing how Americans have responded that we still have the will to be free, and to sacrifice our own lives to keep that freedom. I love this country for that very reason. I'm proud to be an American for that very reason and many more.

But, my question is for us as Christians, How will we respond to this invasion of Evil? Satan would hope that our Faith would crumble like the twin towers, Satan would hope that our Love for people would turn cold because of this act of evil. Satan would hope that our Peace would be turned into fear. Satan hopes to move you away from what you know to be the truth, God's Word, and move you to some other source of comfort.

How will We Respond? The Apostle Paul who knows something about being persecuted for one's faith, who knows about being stoned, being beaten, being boiled in oil, being imprisoned because of his beliefs. The apostle Paul knows what it is to be invaded at every level by evil, and in the end, He knew what it was to Stand Firm in His Faith, To Stand Firm in his Love, To stand firm in His conviction, and His Peace.

Listen to his battle tested words of life.

10 Finally, be strong in the Lord and in his mighty power. 11 Put on the full armor of God so that you can take your stand against the devil's schemes. 12 For our struggle is not against flesh and blood, but against the rulers, against the authorities, against the powers of this dark world and against the spiritual forces of evil in the heavenly realms.

First Sunday

Last week I talked about being filled with the Holy Spirit so you can live a life with Spiritual Power, so you can be effective in the Christian life. Now Paul is instructing us to Stand Firm, and to be Strong in the Lord and in His Mighty power. This power doesn't come from us, it's not a human power, it's not something we can work towards, this power is a gift from God, through his Holy Spirit.

As Christians there are some things we just need to realize as truth. First, as the body of Christ we must be united and built up so we are ready for the invasion of Evil that will come and has come, and every believer needs to be prepared for the fight.

I get the impression that many believers today are under the impression that they somehow don't have to worry about things getting too bad, that somehow they are going to be shielded from all the evil in the world. Christians, we need to have a reality check. Do you realize how many Nazarene Church members died in Tuesday's attack? One of the Pilots in one of those planes was a Nazarene member. We had over 200 members of the Church of the Nazarene that worked in the World Trade Center buildings, and 50 more in the Pentagon. We don't know how many we have lost.

As our Nation has been shaken from its slumber, I pray that the Church is shaken from its sleep, and we will take serious the call to battle, Paul's call to put on the full armor of God so that we can take our stand against the devil's schemes.

When Paul wrote to his readers to be strong in the Lord and in his mighty power, those Greek words used to describe this power is the same power that raised Jesus from the dead, and the same words that described the power to bring them back to life when they were dead in their transgressions and sins. In their minds, there was no doubt that this power was enough for them to have victory in this life.

Do you know this power? On Tuesday, Was God's Power, His Peace evident in your life?

Don't misunderstand me. This power doesn't take away our feelings and our emotions. It doesn't keep us from hurting, from weeping, from feeling all those emotions that we should feel. What this power does for us is keeps us from Despair, From Doubt in God, From Fear.

Friends, We have been invaded. And when you are in battle, you better have on the whole armor, the full protection for your body, and you want to have your full complement of weapons. You also need to know who the enemy is.

Listen to Paul v. 12. 12 For our struggle is not against flesh and blood, but against the rulers, against the authorities,

First Sunday

against the powers of this dark world and against the spiritual forces of evil in the heavenly realms.

How many of you know that there is a Spiritual Battle that rages in the heaven right now as we speak? There is a battle between Good and Evil. Satan wants to destroy you and all of mankind. The only reason he doesn't is because of God's Power and Protection. There are times in our world where we see first hand with our own eyes this battle that is waged between good and evil. The Bible teaches us that Evil was introduced into this world through Sin, and ever since then it has been a curse upon mankind. But we also know that Satan's rule is limited and only for a time.

There is going to be a final battle one of these days. Satan and all the evil forces will wage war against God and his people, Satan will try to destroy and end God's rule.

That Day is not far off my friends. I ask you this morning, Are you ready to Stand? Do you have the Armor of God on, some of you know what the armor of God is, but do you wear the belt of Truth, the Breastplate of Righteousness, are your feet fitted with the gospel of Peace, the helmet of Salvation, the shield of Faith, do you have the Sword of the Spirit, God's Word? Are you armed with these things? A soldier must be ready at all times, because as we found out, we don't know when the enemy might strike. You can't just try to climb into your Armor on Sunday morning and then slip out of it on Sunday evening thinking that will be sufficient, that will spell disaster.

Will You Stand Firm? I can promise you if you will Stand Firm For Jesus Christ, you won't be disappointed. Knowing Jesus Christ as your Personal Savior is the key to standing Firm when the evil one comes.

You may be here this morning, and you may not see the need to be protected, you seem to have it all under control. Let me tell you something, your world can be turned upside down in an instant, and I ask you what will you hold on to that will not crumble if it's not Jesus?

I have to admit I wasn't surprised when I heard the story. But it makes me want to cry. A pastor who has been building a great church, over 100 teenagers, running over 300 people, when just two years ago it was running only in the 50's and 60's much like ours.

He has a wonderful wife, with three great kids, two teenagers. He was busy doing God's work, I'm sure very busy, I'm sure way overloaded with responsibilities. His life was invaded by the evil one, and the problem was when he reached back to fight, he realized he didn't have the Armor of God, he had been too busy to protect himself. Before he knew it, pornography had slipped into his mind and heart and chained him. We don't even know how many casualties his personal sin will cause in the lives of those in

First Sunday

his church, and in his own family. Your personal sin effects the people closest to you. Evil invaded, and he wasn't standing Firm on the foundation of Jesus Christ.
Thank God he is seeking help, and has repented of this tragic sin, but what a price to pay.

What are you holding on to this morning? Is it Jesus? If it's not Jesus let me warn you now, ahead of time, it will fail you when your life is invaded. It's only through knowing Jesus in a personal way will we have the victory.

This morning the battle rages on. On a day not that far from today, there will be the Final battle. Satan will gather his forces, the nations of the World that hate Christianity and all it stands for, the Anti Christ will have had his rule, but then the final chapter will be read in time and space.

Let me read to you the reason we can know that Victory is ours even now, even today.

Rev. 19:11-21
I saw heaven standing open and there before me was a white horse, whose rider is called Faithful and True. With justice he judges and makes war. 12 His eyes are like blazing fire, and on his head are many crowns. He has a name written on him that no one knows but he himself. 13 He is dressed in a robe dipped in blood, and his name is the Word of God. 14 The armies of heaven were following him, riding on white horses and dressed in fine linen, white

and clean. 15 Out of his mouth comes a sharp sword with which to strike down the nations. "He will rule them with an iron scepter." He treads the winepress of the fury of the wrath of God Almighty. 16 On his robe and on his thigh he has this name written:

KING OF KINGS AND LORD OF LORDS.

REV 19:17
And I saw an angel standing in the sun, who cried in a loud voice to all the birds flying in midair, "Come, gather together for the great supper of God, 18 so that you may eat the flesh of kings, generals, and mighty men, of horses and their riders, and the flesh of all people, free and slave, small and great."

REV 19:19
Then I saw the beast and the kings of the earth and their armies gathered together to make war against the rider on the horse and his army. 20 But the beast was captured, and with him the false prophet who had performed the miraculous signs on his behalf. With these signs he had deluded those who had received the mark of the beast and worshiped his image. The two of them were thrown alive into the fiery lake of burning sulfur. 21 The rest of them were killed with the sword that came out of the mouth of the rider on the horse, and all the birds gorged themselves on their flesh.

First Sunday

Friends, that's why you can stand firm today, Jesus is the reason for our Hope. Jesus is the reason for our Peace. Jesus is the reason that in a time like this, We Can Stand. Are you Ready? If you are not, you can come and pray and let God transform your life, and give you the Spirit of Power through his forgiveness and grace.

Rev. Ronald W. Scates

Highland Park Presbyterian Church
Dallas, Texas

Sunday, September 16, 2001

I was all set to launch a sermon series on 9-16 going straight through the Book of Malachi during the fall of 2001 (I am a "lectio continua" preacher, usually preaching straight through books or sections of Scripture). When 9-11 happened, the first thing that popped into my mind was CS Lewis' sermon on "Learning Latin In Wartime"...... the gist of which is that when cataclysmic things happen, we should not jettison what is important and foundational to our lives, thereby diverting all our focus, energy, etc on the current pressing event to the detriment of who we really are, and what we need for the long-haul. I also felt strongly that the Lord had led me to preach this series at this particular time in the life of our congregation; that 9-11 was no surprise to Him, and that what our congregation needed most at this horrific moment was NOT a topical sermon containing my knee-jerk/fallible insights on what 9-11 was all about ..... but we needed to hear what God was saying to us .... and that would most likely happen if I stuck with His Word rather than my wisdom, or lack thereof.

I was uncomfortable going ahead with this strategy .... particularly when I began learning that nearly all my pastor friends were scuttling their planned sermons, and were instead preaching directly about 9-11. I went ahead anyway with beginning the Malachi series. I received some scathing letters in response, most along the lines that I had made the pulpit of HPPC irrelevant that day because I did not focus the sermon only on 9-11. If I had it to do over again, I would do what I did ..... believing that God's Word is never irrelevant .... And is the supreme source for our comfort amidst even life's worst catastrophes.

THE GOD WHO LOVES...AND HATES

Malachi 1: 1-5

Every preacher in America has faced the same question this week. That question is: "What and how to preach in the wake of horrific disaster that had shaken this nation to its very foundations?" We preacher types even asked each other that question. Many of my friends said that they were abandoning their sermons that were planned for today and they were going to speak directly to the issue at hand. I wrestled with doing that, but all week long I was haunted, by a sermon preached by C. S. Lewis, entitled, "Learning Latin in Wartime", where he said that there is a real danger in the midst of crisis, in abandoning what seemed to be the more mundane and yet very important building blocks of humanity, and rushing toward the tyranny of the urgent. He said that Great Britain would emerge more healthy and strong from underneath the barrage of Nazi bombs, if she would continue to learn Latin.

I have decided to go ahead with my planned sermon series, straight through the book of Malachi, one of the so called "minor" prophets, because there are only fifty-five verses in the whole book, and yet forty-seven of those fifty-five verses are in the form of direct address by God to His people. So the book is anything but minor.

In my own brokenness, in the wake of Tuesday's horror, this sermon has taken a different direction than I thought it was going to go last Monday. With all the unknowns that you and I are faced with from this past week, we don't even know who Malachi was. The word in Hebrew means simply "my messenger". Is this a proper name? Or as John Calvin thought, perhaps this is a reference to the prophet, Ezra, in whose time period, about 465-440 B.C., this word came from God to the people of Israel. It comes to them about seventy years after they had returned from the horror of the Babylonian exile. Their nation had been reforged. The temple rebuilt. The sacrificial system restored. Life had taken on once again, a sense of normalcy. And yet, all was not well. And so God raises up Malachi to address the nation of Israel, a people who had lost any sense of passion for, or fear of, Almighty God. And my friends, that is a very, very dangerous place to be spiritually. My hope is that as we go through the book of Malachi, you and I will be averted from going down that same road. As so I invite

First Sunday

you now to turn with me in your Bibles, and keep them open during the sermon, as we begin this sermon series, with Malachi 1: 1-5. Beginning to read at the first chapter of the first verse, this is the Word of God.

An oracle: The Word of the Lord to Israel through Malachi. "I have loved you," says the Lord. "But you ask, 'How have you loved us?'" "Was not Esau Jacob's brother?" the Lord says. "Yet I have loved Jacob, but Esau have I hated, and I have turned his mountains into a wasteland and left his inheritance to the desert jackals." Edom may say,"Though we have been crushed, we will rebuild the ruins." But this is what the Lord Almighty says: "They may build, but I will demolish. They will be called the Wicked Land, a people always under the wrath of the Lord. You will see it with your own eyes and say, 'Great is the Lord-even beyond the borders of Israel!" Join me as we pray.

And now Father, as my words are true to Your Word, may they be taken to heart, but as my words should stray from Your Word, may they be quickly forgotten. Through Jesus Christ our Lord. Amen.

In verse one of our text, we learn that this prophecy of Malachi, is called an "oracle". In Hebrew that word literally means "burden". What an appropriate word for you and me who gather in this place today, burdened, who are weighed down by heavy hearts, broken hearts. As we come here this morning, we hope to hear a word from the Lord, hoping that God will speak to us as clearly as He spoke to the nation of Israel, through the prophet Malachi. Oh, the terror and the numbness has lifted, the rebuilding has begun. Life is beginning to go back to normalcy. I am not talking about us, that will come in time. I am talking about the nation of Israel back in 5th century BC, after they had been carted off in terror to the nation of Babylon. Their temple had been bulldozed. Their nation destroyed. Now they have returned. God has blessed them. He has given them back their homeland. The temple is being rebuilt. Their lives are getting back into the swing of the routine, into normalcy again.

This week, America was brought to its knees, by violent, evil acts of terrorism. But you know what? Being on our knees is not a bad place to be spiritually. This is the week that the wall between church and state fell like twin towers. Packed out prayer services everywhere. This is the week that America went to church. And yet, when the numbness and the terror begins to lift, as it will eventually, will we have a passion for the God and Father of our Lord Jesus Christ? Or will we go back to spiritual business as usual? Just like the nation of Israel. For you see my friends, the burden of this oracle, the real burden, is that God in His magnanimous, inestimable, unfathomable, gracious, unconditional Love that He has for the nation of Israel and for you and me, bears the burden of a nation that has turned its back on Him and who finds His

First Sunday

Gracious Love to be rather ho-hum and routine. And easy to walk away from. You see, the nation of Israel, you might say, after the terror of Babylon, has been gripped by a "post-traumatic stress syndrome". One that we might call - Deus domesticatus. They had traded in the vibrant, Holy God for a vacant hohum God. A domesticated God. A declawed God. For the nation of Israel, God had become like a pet skunk, all of His offensiveness removed, so that, they could easily relegate Him into the bin of convenience, and insignificance. And that is the burden that the heart of God can hardly bear.

In verses two and three of our text, He takes Israel back in history and reminds them of Jacob and Esau. He says, "You want an example, Israel?" Complacent, snide Israel, who says, "God, You've loved us?" For you see, I don't care who you are. I don't care where you come from. I don't care what you've done. I don't care where you are spiritually. Well, I do, but for the sake of the argument, let's say I don't.

Wherever you are. God's first word to you and to me is always a word of love, as He puts forth here in verse two. But snide, complacent Israel says, "Oh, really! You love us. Just how have You done that?" God says, "You want an example? You are of lineage of Jacob. Jacob became Israel. That is what your nation is named after. It was to Jacob that I gave the promise, the covenant promise, that I originally made with Abraham. The promise that you would become a great nation. A promise of land; and that the Messiah would come through your loins. That promise went to Jacob. But by all human rights, all cultural standards, that promise should have gone to Esau. Jacob was not firstborn, Esau was. Esau was the rightful heir to the land, the nation, and the messianic hope. And yet, I have chosen you, O Jacob. Surprise of surprise! In fact, I even have worked through Jacob's sinful treachery. Remember how he scammed his brother for the birthright? I have redeemed even that, O Israel, in order to make you My Chosen People, because I love you, unconditionally. Jacob I have loved. Esau I have hated." Now you and I have just about had a boatload, up to here, of hatred this week. The last thing that we need to do is think about God hating someone. "Please Ron, spare us of this nonsense." You and I, oftentimes, make a big mistake, when we approach a text, a verse like verse three, that just grates on us. We make a mistake when we begin to anthropomorphize God. We lay our human trip on Him. We project our sinful, fallen, human characteristics on God. When you and I hate, it is always a sinful mixture, of abuse and evil prejudice. But God is Holy. God is righteous. God is sinless.

The Hebrews knew all about love and hate. There is Hebrew hyperbole here. They use those terms in a sense of inheritance. When a son would inherit from a father, he was called "loved". The other sons, that did not inherit, was called "hated". It had nothing to do with emotions. It

First Sunday

simply meant chosen or not chosen. To be loved was to be chosen for the promise, the inheritance. To be hated was to not be chosen. Does God hate? Sure, God hates. God hates injustice and evil and terrorism and grief and racism. In fact, God hates those things with a passion so much that He was willing to hang on a cross for that kind of hatred. The hatred that you and I have been victims of this week. And dare we say that hatred that we oftentimes surprisingly find welling up in the shadows and darkness of our own souls?

Here in the context of this passage, it simply means "Jacob I have chosen to be my chosen people. Esau, whose lineage would go on to be the nation of Edom, I have not chosen to be my chosen people. Jacob I have loved and Esau I have hated." In fact, Edom would go on to be a nation that would turn its back totally on God. Would totally turn its back on its brother Israelites. In fact, when the Israelites were carried off in Babylonian terror, the Edomites cashed in on that. They would spend the rest of their existence under the wrath of God's justice.

How then, in the wake of this past Tuesday, ought you and I to read verse four of our text? "We have been crushed, but we will rebuild." That sounds like a pretty good battle cry to throw in the face of Osama bin Laden. In fact, that became Edom's motto. "Oh, God, may not have chosen us, and that may crush us, but we will rebuild." My friends, that is sheer presumptuousness on the part of Edom. It can be sheer presumptuousness on the part of America as well. If we think, "All we have got to do in the midst of this crisis, is to dig down deep; that it's the American spirit that can save us; that it is the American dream that will rise to the surface here. With our military might, our economic wealth and affluence, we can rebuild." What are we going to rebuild? Are we going to rebuild twin towers, that point the world to our affluence and materialism, or are we going to retain a passion for God and put God in His rightful place? But, we can't put God in His rightful place, He is there whether we think He is or not. When people say, "Make Jesus Lord of your life." I say, "You can't do that." Jesus *is* Lord. What you need to do is recognize it.

If we think we can rebuild on our own strength, by our own military or economic or political might, we have bought into the fallacy of Edom.

How will you rebuild your life? How will I rebuild my life out of this horrible tragedy that has occurred? That is, when the numbness and the terror lifts, as it will. Will we begin to drift back into spiritual business as usual? Or will we be able to say in the words of verse five of our text, above everything else, "Great is the Lord." Beyond the borders of Israel, beyond the borders of the United States of America. A family pulled up to a red light and a bee flew in the window and was buzzing all around, trying to get out through the windshield. They didn't want to kill it. They just wanted to get him out of the car. They were

First Sunday

trying to swat him toward the open windows. He refused to cooperate. He just became madder. And he terrorized them all the way home. They got home. The dad pulled the car up next to some flowering vines. They rolled the windows down. They felt maybe if the bee sniffed the flowers, he would head out the windows and they would be OK. He would be OK. The next morning, they came down to find out what had happened to their little buzzing friend and they found him dead on the back panel of the car, beneath the rear window. That bee thought he knew how to get out of this jamb. He spent all night ramming himself into that back window, determined by his strength, and by his knowledge that he could get out of that car, when all the time, the windows were down, and the sweet fragrance of flowers was filling the car.

My friends, as we stand on the brink of a war that we have never seen the likes of before in humankind (I am not trying to be an alarmist, but I do not know what is going to happen, but I do know that everything is different). Everything is changed. If we think, we can just pull ourselves up by our red, white, and blue bootstraps, that it's the American way that can lead us through this, then we are no different than Edom and Israel. We will learn a hard lesson. Jesus Christ is King of Kings and Lord of Lords. He alone is The Way, The Truth, and The Life. God have mercy on us. God have mercy on the United States of America, should we think that there is any other way.

Join me as we pray.

Lord God, remove from our hearts any false bravado. All those things that we think can save us Lord outside of You. Lord, we throw ourselves on your mercy. We cling to You, because You are a God who saves. Through Jesus Christ our Lord.

Amen.

First Sunday

Rev. Jim Standiford

First United Methodist Church
San Diego, CA

Sunday, September 16, 2001

I remember praying, praying, and praying some more, then attempting to pick scripture passages that I thought might help the congregation in a time of deep need. I wanted to give them something in their faith to hold on to for strength.

Our congregation, in cooperation with several others, held an interfaith service on the evening of September 11. These two events, the interfaith service and then our Sunday service on the next weekend when I preached the above sermon, were both very well received and seemed to give the people a sense of stability in the chaos of the time.

We also offered special services after the devastating fires of our area in 2003 and 2007. All of these events pushed people to consider their faith, and the response of the church seemed to be a source of strength for them. God is the one who will judge if the preaching and the services and our living was faithful. We pray in gratitude always, because God is gracious.

Donald Robert Elton & Aura Agudo Elton

GOD'S PROMISES

Isaiah 41:5-10   John 12:12-15

Eternal God, pour out your Spirit upon us that we might be sensitive to your presence in our midst, that we might be attentive to your Word, and that we might be faithful always to your way, through Jesus Christ our Lord we pray. Amen.

"The Lord is my shepherd I shall not want." "Come unto me all who labor and are heavy laden, and I will give you rest."

We all need rest right now, don't we? We need rest because we have seen the valley of the shadow of death in the crumbled, twisted masses that are now the canyons of Lower Manhattan. The part of that great city which once was marked by twin towers standing tall, strong, and true, now has a profile of posters, a great patchwork of posters on almost every wall, with the headline "Missing" above, and then a picture or a description of a loved one. That is what marks the city now.

We are in need of rest because we hurt deep inside. Our first reaction was one of grief, one of unbelieving. Our first reaction was one of horror, one of tears, one of holding anyone who was around us. Our first reaction was to want to turn off the television, to close our eyes, to make it all go away somehow, and say, let's go back to Tuesday

First Sunday

morning and start all over again. Yet we couldn't turn off the television. We couldn't pull ourselves away. We were afraid of what the next moment might bring, and we wanted to be there.

After the horror, the anguish, and the pain, then came anger, and justifiably so. These are acts that deserve anger. For anyone to make of another human being, let alone almost three hundred other human beings, living missiles of death and destruction is an unspeakable evil. It is an evil beyond our words, beyond our comprehending. We are justified in our anger.

Over the last decade almost every terrorist activity throughout the world has been committed by some militant, fundamentalist, religious group or individual. These are people who take the essence of their faith tradition, whatever it may be, and they twist it beyond recognition. They give themselves absolute power and authority to do as they please.

As you well know, every evidence points that this is the mastermind of one or at least a small band of Islamic militant fundamentalists. Please, dear friends, this is not Islam. This is a deviant, far branch of Islam. Islam stands for peace. Islam stands for the universal brotherhood of all humankind. Islam is one of the great historical religions of our world. We want to affirm our Islamic brothers and sisters, but we cannot affirm what has happened.

They are not alone. There are Jewish militant fundamentalists as well. Jewish militant fundamentalists take the tradition of the Hebrew people and twist it beyond recognition. A number of years ago it was Jewish militant fundamentalists that bombed a mosque at the time of prayer, when the building was filled with people all on their knees, with their heads touching the ground. It was the Jewish militant fundamentalists that several years ago killed the then Prime Minister of Israel because he would not agree with their ideas.

But as Christian people we too are guilty.

There are within the realm of Christianity those who are militant fundamentalists. They have taken the teachings of Jesus and twisted them beyond recognition. They are the ones who fight each other in Northern Ireland. They are the ones who kill gay and lesbian people in this nation. They are the ones who bomb medical clinics. They are the ones who kill doctors who may have as a part of their practice performing abortions.

The enemy is militant fundamentalism when it somehow gives people the concept that they are in control and not God, and that they have the right to decide who has life and who does not. The enemy is that person or that group that says I am right and everyone else is wrong. They are the ones who say, if you do not agree with us, then you

First Sunday

have no right to live. These are the people who believe that only a very few have the truth and everyone else is wrong, and creation will be better if all the rest are gone. So they massacre.

Let there be no mistake. That which was done this week is an unspeakable evil. We must pray and we must work with all of our energy for justice. Those who are culpable must be held accountable. There is no doubt about that. And yet we must be very careful. We must be careful not to react out of our anger. We must be careful not to act out in vengeance. Because if we do, then there will be uncontrolled anger released and many more innocent people will die. We must pray and work for justice.

Rose Marie Berger is a Catholic social worker in Washington, D.C. She said on Tuesday morning at 5:00 a.m. she was awaken by a strong voice calling her to prayer. She got up and opened up her Book of Hours. The passage that was before her was this. "Everyday rest your arms upon the window sill of heaven and gaze upon God. Then when your heart is full of that vision, turn with strength for the day." She said, "I was so grateful for that time of prayer, because when I turned to my day, my day was filled with hell. If it had not been for the vision of heaven that I had in my heart, I would have been overcome by the evil that was loosed in the world."

That is what you and I need to remember friends. Unless we have heaven in our hearts, the evil of the world can overcome us. We need to center ourselves in God, and in God's strength, and in God's grace, so that we can be a positive influence in this world, and so we can witness to the world the goodness of God in the land of the living.

Let us turn and look at the scriptures for this morning, scriptures that I chose for this day. The first is from the prophet Isaiah in the Old Testament. It is a court scene in which God is trying the nations of the world. The reason God is trying the nations is because they have turned to idolatry. The usual image that we have of idolatry is people sitting around making little images, instead of worshiping God. But that is just a symbol of what it is. Idolatry is worshiping values that are contrary to the values of God. Idolatry is worshiping the work of our own hands, instead of worshiping God. That is what the terrorists are doing. They are worshiping the work of their own hands, their hatreds. That is idolatry. To the people of Israel in Isaiah's day, Isaiah paints a picture of this court scene. God says, "In these other nations that have fallen away, people help other people. It looks good from the outside, until you realize they help other people to do evil. In these other nations brother encourages brother, and artisan encourages the goldsmith. Those who hammer upon the metal encourage each other. All that looks wonderful, until you realize everything that is going on in those nations is for

First Sunday

evil." Then God says, "Israel, I am your help. I am your strength."

Friends, this word was written to the nation of Israel when they were being held prisoners of war in Babylon, the rogue nation of the world in that day. This word was written to Israel when it was in its greatest time of need. Hear the words that God speaks to people in need. "Do not fear, I am your God; do not fear, I will be with you; I will be your strength, I will be your help, I will uphold you with my victorious right arm." Those are the words not only for Israel in Isaiah's time, those are the words for all of God's people in this time. Those are the promises of God.

I am sure that amongst your prayers this week there has been a word, "Oh God, why didn't you do something? Why didn't you change things?" I have prayed that, and I know better. It is a part of who we are; we want things to be different. Oh, if we could only turn the clock back to 5:00 a.m. on Tuesday. But God does not abrogate God's natural law. It's a part of creation. It is in that part of creation and that natural law that you and I have free will. Otherwise if God were to intervene and to change things along the way, you and I would become nothing but puppets. We would not be free. We would not have life in any sense that we know it now.

What God does do is come in our midst and live with us. We know that most clearly in the life of Jesus. He came to people who were hungry. He came to people in pain. He came to people who were dying. He came to people who were grieving. He came to people who were alone, who were afraid, and he was with them. That is the witness of our God.

So where was God on Tuesday morning? God was sitting with those people on those hijacked airliners, comforting them. God was in the crumbling buildings as they fell to the ground. God was beside the rescue workers as they dug through the rubble. God was with them when they were crushed. That is where God always is, in the hurting and painful places of life.

In the passage from the Gospel of John, we have a little view of what is a very familiar picture, the Palm Sunday parade. John writes it differently than the other gospel writers. We see the great crowd and hear them cry out, "Hosanna, blessed is he who comes in the name of the Lord!" Remember the word "hosanna," means "come and save us." For someone to be "blessed in the name of the Lord," means that they have the authority of God. So the cry of the people as John understands it, is these people are crying out for Jesus to come with military might and save them, to throw off the oppressors of Rome. But John makes it very clear it is after Jesus hears the cry of the people that he chooses his vehicle for entering the city. He

First Sunday

doesn't choose a horse, or a chariot. He chooses a donkey. He chooses the symbol of service, of humility, and of peace. This is the nature of God's help in our midst. God comes as one who is in our midst to help us, to serve us, by giving God's life to us. We know that in our Lord and Savior Jesus Christ.

So how is God acting out God's promises now? You have seen them all about you, haven't you? You have seen them on television. You have probably seen them in your own neighborhood. Let me lift up just a couple.
The other morning on television there was woman who was interviewed named Diane Leonard. Her husband Dan was killed in the Oklahoma City bombing. Out of her grief she went on television to speak to those who were suffering now because of the loss of loved ones. She spoke a word of hope and understanding to them. She said the most important thing for you to do was to hold on to the family you have now. The next most important thing for you to do is to support the rescue workers. Know that those people aren't doing a job; they are on a mission, a mission to save life. She said to be patient with yourself, and be patient with the rescue workers. They are working as hard and as long and as fast as humanly possible. Know that they have your best interests at heart. Here is this woman, wounded herself, speaking out of her grief to help others. She is the promise of God at work.

Donald Robert Elton & Aura Agudo Elton

I was a part of the interfaith service Tuesday night at St. Paul's Episcopal Cathedral. There were several poignant moments in the midst of the service. One of those came when a Jewish rabbi, a Muslim Imam, and an Anglican bishop of Palestinian background together lifted the flame to the paschal candle and lit it. The candle is a symbol of the presence of God in our midst. The candle is a symbol of new life. These three persons of these three divergent traditions came together and did that symbolic act. Friends, in our lives may it not be a symbol, may it be reality, that with our brothers and sisters of other religious traditions, we give witness by the way we live to the presence of God in life.

Another poignant moment was when the Imam spoke. He said on Tuesday morning he had received a phone call right after the towers had been hit. The phone call was from his next-door neighbor, who is a Roman Catholic woman. Her question was, "What can we do to help protect your mosque?" That is the promise of God at work in our lives.

St. Paul, writing to the Ephesians, tells them to gear up for war, to gear up for the war of the spirit. He says to them, "Put on the belt of truth. Put on the breastplate of righteousness. As for your feet, put on anything that will help you proclaim the gospel of peace. Pick up the shield of faith. Put on the helmet of salvation. Take hold of the sword of the spirit, which is the Word of God. With the full

First Sunday

armor of God go into battle." That is the clarion call to you and me this day as Christian people. With the full armor of God we are to go into battle for goodness and righteousness in our world.

Let me close with this. There was a young boy who was quite ill in the hospital. His pastor visited him, and said, "Have you ever prayed the 23rd Psalm?" The little boy said, "No." The pastor said, "Let me suggest you do it this way. You hold up your hand and with your fingers you pray 'The...Lord...is...my...shepherd.' And you do it over and over again, saying a word for each finger so you measure them out and you hear each one, 'The...Lord...is...my... shepherd.'"

That evening the boy's father came to visit him. He told his father about the pastor's visit and about the prayer. But he said, "Dad, that's not me, so I changed the prayer. I changed it this way because, Dad, I am not in this alone. You and mom are helping me. The doctors and nurses are helping me. My friends at school are helping me. My friends at church are helping me. I changed the prayer to be like this. 'The... Lord...is...our...shepherd.'"

During the night that young man died. The nurses found him early in the morning. His arms were on top of the sheet of the bed. He was holding on to the our finger. "The... Lord...is...our...shepherd." Dear friends, hold on to that.

Thanks be to God.

Amen.

First Sunday

Rev. Andrew Stirling

Timothy Eaton Memorial Church
Toronto, Ontario, Canada

Sunday, September 16, 2001

It was September 12, 2001, and my wife and I were still on vacation in the United States getting ready for our drive back home across the border to Canada. We were staying in Portsmouth, N.H. and as the day developed and the sheer impact of what had happened the day before entered our consciousness, I decided now was the time to write my sermon for the next Sunday. I sat in an outside coffee shop near the centre of the historic seaport and with the bible open and a copy of the New York Times and the Boston Globe in hand, I began to craft my words. I only had one thing in my mind, "How can I bring the Word of God to bear upon this situation?" I also felt the passion of a pastor for their people. "What word can bring comfort and guidance in a time such as this?" With these questions burning in my heart, I began to write...

It was obvious from the attendance the next Sunday that the impact of the events of 9-11 was enormous. Regardless of which side of the border one lived on, the feeling that we were entering a dangerous era of uncertainty was pervasive. The congregation had known that I had been in the United States during the attack and they were relieved to see me home in safety. More than that, however, they needed a word of encouragement. Because Canada had been at the forefront of helping stranded Americans when the airports were closed, a special bond had developed between our two countries and in some ways, my people wanted that to be expressed. Also, Canadians had lost their lives and one of our members was in the World Trade Center during the attack attending a banking conference and had seen people jump from high offices and landed next to him, so there was mourning and grieving. I believe the sermon helped place everything within the framework of the Gospel and the worship around the sermon was comforting and prophetic. I was also overwhelmed by correspondence from radio listeners who tune in to our broadcast. Many were even frightened to leave their own homes and desperately needed some hope to hold on to.

I have very mixed feelings about the current situation. On a positive note there has clearly been such an emphasis on security that we have not seen in North America, a similar terrorist attack, despite the fact that they have been attempted. We should be grateful for this blessing. The world is also more aware of Islam and its teachings and there is a greater level of understanding although we struggle with its complexity and diversity.

However, the aftermath of 9-11 has resulted in wars on two fronts in Afghanistan and Iraq and has cost billions of dollars. In addition many lives have been lost and the

First Sunday

spread of Muslim extremism has not abated in parts of the world. From the point of view of the church, there was clearly an upsurge in attendance for a while afterwards but Christians and nominal believers have once again slipped into their apathy, materialism and spirit of inwardness. In many ways I am disappointed because I felt that 9-11 gave the world an opportunity to turn more fervently to God and to seek the peace of His Son Jesus. The dream needs to be reclaimed!

In Search of... Healing

John 5:1-15

It was an idyllic New England day. The night before there had been some slight rains and the mist of the early morning was hovering at the foot of the beautiful, Vermont, Green Mountains. As the sun began to rise and burn off the mist, the emerald green mountains of Vermont seemed brighter than any jewelry I had ever seen in my life. It was a glorious morning.

Marial and I were driving on Route 30 from Manchester Center to Brattleboro, one of the most serene and peaceful and gorgeous parts of that free and fair land. The air had a chill to it and, as the sun warmed it, we thoroughly enjoyed the freedom of America.

After a while, having driven along that beautiful route, we switched on the radio to find out what the weather would be for the rest of the day and we heard the most ridiculous thing that we had ever heard in our lives: that planes had flown into the World Trade Center: that the Pentagon might have been bombed. It sounded like one of those silly hoaxes that morning shows often air in the United States. There was only one difference: the voice delivering the news was familiar. It was a Canadian voice. It was Peter Jennings, and it was real.

In a state of shock, we continued to drive through the mountains, although their beauty seemed to have lost its hue and its glow. I pulled over into a gas station just outside of the town of Keene. When I was there, the woman who was to take my money was weeping uncontrollably. The mechanics had put down their tools and their greasy hands were grasping their cups of coffee like they had never clasped their cups of coffee before. There was an eerie silence and I realized the world would never be the same.

We drove on quietly to our final destination of Portsmouth, New Hampshire. As we got near the port city, there were police cars around the road. The place had been cordoned off and we were forced to go down a side road. We just drove and drove, we knew not where, in an area that was normally beautiful but now, because of what had happened in New York and Washington, everything had changed. It no longer seemed beautiful. We pulled into our hotel and

First Sunday

on the faces of all the people that we saw, there was shock, disbelief.

I thought of the words of Winston Churchill on October 5th, 1938, after a peace accord had been signed with Hitler. He said this: "We have sustained defeat without a war."

Indeed, a defeat had permeated the whole land. It would never be the same.

In the editorial in the New York Times the next morning, the editor wrote these words, and they summed up how I was feeling on that morning: "We look back at sunrise yesterday through pillars of smoke and dust, down streets snowed under with the atomized debris of the skyline, and we understand that everything has changed."

But it had not only changed the United States of America. It had not only changed the southern part of Manhattan. It had not only changed Washington, D.C. In fact, what happened last Tuesday had changed the whole world.

That very Tuesday, a panic beset my heart. I realized that a very good friend of mine who had been in church the very week before, here at Eaton Memorial, was attending a conference of international bankers at the World Trade Center and I realized that he must have been there; a friend whom I had known for 15 years, who wrote the foreword of my second book - that's how close a friend he is. I tried all day and all evening to phone his wife. Finally I got through and found out that he had been in the building, that he had been evacuated minutes before the second plane crashed, but that he had stood at the bottom of the building and saw people jump from 30 and 40 stories high.

I realized the world would never be the same. I echo the words of our Prime Minister, Jean Chrétien, who in his magnificent speech on Friday said that it is not only just our neighbors who have suffered this but our family, our family. And not only our family, I would go even further. I would agree with those who say that what happened at the World Trade Center was a crime against the whole of humanity. Indeed, humanity as a whole will never be the same because of what happened on that fateful day, on Tuesday, September 11, 2001.

But one thing that is not changing is the word of God. As I sat on Tuesday night and thought, "What on earth am I going to say on Sunday morning - Should I change my text? Should I pick something else?" - I began to read the passage of the story of the healing of the man at Bethesda and realized that what the world needs more than anything at this very moment is healing; and that the encounter between the man at the pool at Bethesda and Jesus of Nazareth has lessons for us and for the whole world about the nature and the power of God's healing. For in that encounter, there is a word for the whole of humanity which

First Sunday

we need to carry in our hearts at this time in which our world has changed.

The first thing that we find in this encounter between Jesus and the man at Bethesda was a challenge. The man had been a paralytic and he had sat by that pool for a very long time. Jesus says to this man a very strange phrase. He says: "Do you want to be healed? Do you want it?" In other words: Are you willing to believe the things that will bring about your healing?

Now, on the surface, that might seem ridiculous; but it is not. For indeed, in being healed, this man's whole life would have to change. For years, he had sat by the pool with his friends. No longer would he do so. For years, he depended on the sympathy and the kindness of others to help him into the pool, but that would never be the same. For years, he depended on others, but now, he would have to take responsibility for himself. Everything would change. For years he had been passive and simply waited. Now he would be transformed and would have to act. His life would change. Jesus says to him then, clearly: "Do you really want to be healed?"

I think that the world in which we live asks itself that very same question - Do we really want to be healed? - because in many ways, our lives have been shattered by what has occurred. We will always be different because of this week.

Donald Robert Elton & Aura Agudo Elton

One of the things that will make us different is that our complacency is gone. We have just assumed that we who live in North America, this continent of freedom, will not be touched by the evil vicissitudes of this world; that we will be protected by our military power; that we will be protected by our wealth and affluence: that we will be protected by our form of law and order. In many ways, there has been an arrogance about that protection and that freedom.

When others have died in Kosovo or in Rwanda, when buildings have been blown up in Ireland or in my hometown of Manchester, England, when people have been killed on the streets of Sierra Leone, when people have been attacked in Kenya, it has seemed a remote thing.

But now it is no longer remote. We cannot be passive anymore. We cannot hide behind a veneer of our own protection as if somehow we are invulnerable, for our lives are now forever changed.

Derrick Jackson, writing on the Op Ed page of the Boston Globe on Wednesday, put it so prophetically:

It is the most bewildering moment because we have the world's mightiest army, yet the Pentagon was bombed. It is bewildering because America is the world's richest nation, yet its greatest twin symbols of capitalism no longer stand.

First Sunday

It is bewildering because the President says terrorism will not stand, yet he knows not where the enemy stands. ...

It is bewildering because in a nation so numb to celluloid violence, gun violence, and even genocide abroad, no-one can now be detached from the effects of violence.

How right Derrick Jackson is. The shock that was felt around the world is that we are indeed all vulnerable. There is nothing that we can create that can protect us completely and utterly and totally and even eternally.

Many people throughout this period of complacency and peace that we have enjoyed for so long have turned their backs often on religion, or on God, or on faith, or on helping others, or on caring for the world, in the thought that somehow their world is safe. But it is no longer safe. The world is forever changed.

The questions, therefore, that reside in our hearts are: "Are we willing to accept that? Are we willing to be healed?"

The second thing that happens in the encounter between Jesus and the man at the pool of Bethesda is a conflict. When Jesus healed the man at Bethesda, there were those who took exception to Jesus' healing. There were those who said: "You can't do this. You are asking him to pick up his bed and walk on the Sabbath. This is an affront."

There were those who said: "You can't do this. Jesus of Nazareth, who are you? What right do you have to bring healing?"

And so often, my friends, when there is healing, when God does act, when God does try and save, there is conflict. Oh, there have been those who have said over the last few days that God is responsible for this; that God maybe is the one who is, as I mentioned last week, a pernicious God who is out to get them.

But I agree with something that Rev. John Harries said this morning to the children as he ministered to them here on the steps of this church. He said: "No, God is there bringing healing. God is there with those who climbed the stairs to try and save. God is there with those who gave their lives."

But the problem is, the religious traditions of people often seem to supersede the divine healing of God, because we place our traditions above the revelation of the God who is the God of Life. And it doesn't matter what religion it is. We all do it, and we all create our traditions. And out of those traditions, we deny the power and the life-giving spirit of God, because we think that the religion that we mould is more important. Sometimes we deny healing and we have conflict because of our superstitions.

First Sunday

One of the things that made the pool of Bethesda so great was that there were people who felt that if they went into this pool they were automatically healed by its waters. They believed that the divine, little gods that were there around that pool, that were local to that pool, would bring healing and salvation. These people did not have faith in God. They had superstitions. Superstitions that they had built up and had clouded their hearts and their minds to the truth of Jesus of Nazareth who was in their midst on God's behalf to bring healing.

One of the things that astounds me the most is that some of the people who have perpetrated this violence have done so out of superstition, not faith. They believed that they would receive divine glory in Paradise if they enter into a holy war and kill innocent men and women and children. They believed that they would be blessed by God by taking human life. This is superstition. It is not the heart of true religion. It is not the heart of true Islam. It is not the heart of true Judaism and it certainly isn't the heart of true Christianity. In fact, that kind of superstition is evil.

Three times, George Bush in his speech to the nation on Tuesday night, described what happened as evil. Let's be under absolutely no misapprehension. What happened in New York and in Washington was an act of unmitigated evil. It was not the work of the God who, as Jesus said, comes to bring life. It is the thief who comes to kill and to steal and to destroy, but Jesus says: "I have come that you might have life and might have it abundantly."

In secret places, men and women plot their evil. Men and women are in conflict with the healing and life-giving and sustaining power of God. The ultimate idolatry is to take human life and to do it in God's name. That was the idolatry of the Nazis. That is what many of them said. That is the idolatry that I have seen over the years in many different places, that in the name of God, human life is taken - innocent. That is not faith. That is not trust in the God of the Universe. That is superstition and it kills. Jesus saw it eye to eye when he brought healing to that man at Bethesda and even though he was healed, there were those who wanted to criticize the Lord of Life.

But there is also in this passage a great command. Jesus said to the man at Bethesda: [paraphrase] "I want you now to get off your bed and I want you to walk. I want you, as an act of faith, not just to sit here by this pool. I want you to get up on your feet and I want you to get out there. I want you to show that you believe. I want you to demonstrate that you have been healed."

Faith is not some passive thought that somehow everything is just going to work out nicely. Faith is fiducia. It is trust. It is an act of faith. It is stepping out and doing something in God's name in the knowledge that Jesus Christ our Lord goes with us.

First Sunday

My friends, this world that as of this week has forever changed must now do something. I would suggest it needs to do four things:

The first is, it needs to carry out its act of justice. Let us not be under any misapprehension. The people who carried out this deed did so willingly, and they did so knowingly, and they did so wantonly. Any sense of justice would suggest that those people must be held accountable. Those people who did this, if they were to murder a man or a woman on the street, would have to be brought to justice. But justice demands that evidence must always be able to substantiate the charge. Justice suggests that it must always be carried out, not in a spirit of anger, or revenge, but in a spirit of righteousness and truth; that the punishment must fit the crime; that there is no point in the wanton taking of innocent lives to appease our own consciences, for in so doing, those who died in that building and who lie in the rubble will only have had their misery compounded as we bring it on others who are innocent, who will also lie in rubble.

Having said that, to do nothing, to not go after the perpetrators is unjust. In the name of the God of Justice, they must be brought to trial, they must be called to account. Just as Milosevic was in Yugoslavia, so, too, the people who did this must be brought to justice.

The second thing that the world must do is act together. This is not a time for any form of unilateralism on the part of the United States or, indeed, on the part of Canada and the United States. This has been an affront to the whole world and the whole world must act.

Anthony Lewis in the Op Ed page of the New York Times on Wednesday wrote these words:

It is essential, too, that our foreign policy from here on forward eschew any impression of unilateralism. Even our allies have seen an administration uninterested in what others think, ready to impose its views. President Bush would do well to adopt a tone recognizing that America cannot assure security by itself. ...

We, and the world, are looking for words that can bring us together against evil.

Anthony Lewis is right. What happened at the World Trade Center and at the Pentagon is an affront to the whole of humanity and all the nations of the world should be indignant, and all of the world together should oppose this act of terror. This is no time for us to build walls around ourselves, but to build alliances for the sake of a safer world.

The third thing that is needed is a spirit of religious tolerance. More wars have been fought in the history of the

First Sunday

world on the basis of religion than on almost anything else. God's name has been invoked by the sword and the shield too many times and the retribution that we bring against people of faith is something that really must stop for the sake of the world.

I am a Christian. I believe in the unique claims of Jesus Christ. I believe him to be God incarnate, the Word made flesh, the Life and the Truth and the Way. And because I believe him to be that, and because I believe that his way is a way of peace: because I believe that the cross is the ultimate symbol of God's acceptance of humanity as well as God's rejection of sin, I believe that that cross is magnanimous and those arms are open.

I believe, therefore, that we have to work with people of other faiths. I believe that God speaks in many ways through Islam and of course through Judaism. I believe that as people of faith in one God, we have a common responsibility to act together.

Every morning you may not know this, I go to a coffee shop and in that coffee shop there are people from all over the world. I sit shoulder by shoulder with Hindus from India, and Muslims from Lebanon, and Armenians from Lebanon, and the Orthodox from Greece. When I go in in the morning with my clerical collar on, there is a universal "Good Morning, Fahder, Good Morning Father," and we talk about many things. My sitting down with them at a table and having coffee does not compromise my faith in Jesus Christ.

But when I see people pointing the finger at other faiths, then I see my faith challenged. As this world gets smaller, the need for us to get along is greater. I believe Jesus wants that and we bear witness to it.

I think the fourth thing that we must do is to ask ourselves why people hate. What conditions exist in the world that cause people in their heart of hearts to want to take the life of another?

Oh, there will always be madmen. There will always be the insane, the fanatics, the irrational. There will always be crazy people who will do things for no reason at all. But there are also people who do things out of a sense of indignation. Those who have much, I believe, need to ask those who have little: "How might we help, in the name of Jesus Christ?"

When that man was healed, Jesus said something very strange to him. He said: "I want to make sure that you don't keep on sinning, lest this happen again." My friends, I think we need to ask ourselves deep in our hearts: "Let us not sin in trying to resolve this problem."

On that first night in my hotel room in Portsmouth, I realized that I had done a silly thing. I had left my Bible at

First Sunday

home and so I opened the night table drawer next to my bed and there, in a bright red cover, was the Gideons' Bible. God bless them!

I didn't know what to read. I thought: "What on earth, Lord, can I say? I am so filled with anger. I want revenge. I want those who have taken those innocent lives to suffer." I think we all felt that way, did we not? But in the light of day, and in the light of God, I want those who are the perpetrators to be called to justice.

But I want what the Word of God wants. I read from the Book of Romans: Let love be without hypocrisy. Abhor what is evil. Cling to what is good. Be devoted to one another in brotherly love. Give preference to one another in honor, not lagging behind in diligence, fervent in spirit, serving the Lord, rejoicing in hope, persevering in tribulation, devoted to prayer, contributing to the needs of the saints, practicing hospitality. Bless those who persecute you. Bless and not curse. Rejoice with those who rejoice. Weep with those who weep. Never pay back evil for evil to anyone. Respect what is right in the sight of all men and if possible, so far as it depends on you, be at peace with all men.

This is the Word of God.
Amen.

Rev. Jack Wyman

East Hampton Bible Church
East Hampton, CT

September 16, 2001

Ironically, the previous Sunday, I had preached a message on Joy. I was in a series from the Psalms. Interestingly enough, I was scheduled to preach from the 73rd Psalm on September 16. I knew immediately that I must devote the entire message to the attack. I assumed every minister in America would be doing this, or at least that was my hope. I also knew that while the attack would be my only topic, I would not preach topically. I preach nearly always expositionally, anchoring the message in a text. I kept to Psalm 73. I weaved the extraordinary tragic events of the previous week into the passage. And while I have always prepared and used in the pulpit an extensive manuscript, that week I wrote the sermon out word for word and read it nearly verbatim as I had written it. I wanted this message especially to stand the test of time. That morning, there was a stillness and an attentiveness in the congregation that I've never experienced in nearly four decades of preaching. Everyone there wanted to hear a distinct word from God -- and needed to hear it."My prayer and hope was that in this message, the people would find strength, comfort and encouragement.

First Sunday

Our church was in Connecticut, less than a two-hour drive from the site of the first attacks. So this was truly a case of hitting close to home. Incredibly, the son of one of our church members had just walked through the lobby of the World Trade Center. He saw the first jet crash and immediately telephoned his mother. I opened my sermon with this account. It is difficult, even now, to say for certain how the congregation was influenced by the message. At the close of the service, everyone was subdued but genuinely appreciative. We were all sad and still in shock. Yet I also sensed a profound love and unity that day. I decided, over the coming weeks, to preach a series of messages on the biblical issues related to the attack, including grief, patriotism, blame, testimony, and gratitude. The congregation needed and welcomed these clarifying messages.

We have all been reminded since that day that crisis and tragedy rivet and unite our nation as few things do. The minister's task in the pulpit at such intervals never diminishes. At that very sad and uncertain time in our nation's history, God's people needed to know that God and His Word are eternal and unchanging. The world has not grown safer or any more predictable over the past decade. Today, as on September 11, 2001, we must turn to God in faith, rest assured in his love, remain comforted by His promises, and rely in courage upon His sovereign Lordship. This will never change.

Donald Robert Elton & Aura Agudo Elton

Response to Crisis: When Good Things Happen to Bad People: Making Sense of the Senseless

Psalms 73

He was, on this morning, a young man in a hurry. Preoccupied with an important meeting, he skipped up the escalator two steps at a time. At the top he made a quick left and hurriedly exited the door of the World Trade Center out onto the street. He glanced at his watch: a few minutes past 8:30, Tuesday.

A green light at three intersections. Good! This will help, he thought. He was making his way to his office at Salomon, Smith, Barney on Greenwich Street when the unusual sound of a low-flying jet diverted his attention to the sky. What he witnessed next would never, ever be forgotten -- seared in his memory by a mind that tried to tell his eyes they were lying. He grabbed his cell phone and called his mother. His voice was so excited, she hardly recognized it. "Mom," he told her, "This isn't on the news yet, but it will be! An airplane just crashed into one of the World Trade Center towers!"

Daniel Johnson, son of Len and Lin Johnson, and a member of this church, had just witnessed the first in a quick series of the most catastrophic events in American history. It was 8:48AM, Tuesday, September 11, 2001. A date none of us will ever forget. Daniel will tell his

First Sunday

grandchildren what he saw. For the rest of us, the news came over television, or, in my case, over the radio. We glued our eyes and ears. It stunned us, not just once, but over and over again.

A second jumbo jet -- a 767 -- slammed into the South tower of the World Trade Center. A third commercial airliner crashed into the Pentagon in Alexandria, Virginia, outside Washington. Then came news of still a fourth jet, crashing just south of Pittsburgh, amid reports that it was headed for the White House or the US Capital.

But the horror wasn't over yet. First one, and then the other, of the Trade Center towers crumbled to the ground in a hideous cloud of smoke and fire.

The attack upon America by nameless and cowardly terrorists this past week was unprecedented in its destruction, unimaginable in its scope, unyielding in its hatred, unfathomable in its evil and unmitigated in its tragedy and its grief. Its horror staggers the human imagination.

More than 5,000 people are dead, including all passengers and crew aboard four commercial jets, hundreds of policemen and firefighters, including the fire chief of New York City, the deputy fire chief and the beloved chaplain of the New York City fire department -- entire units wiped out. And thousands lie this morning under hundreds of thousands of tons of steel and concrete rubble that was once the proud citadel of American economic power. The World Trade Center, which has graced the New York City skyline since the 1970s, is now only a memory.

The terrorists, not content with that destruction and death, have also assaulted the symbol of American military power, the Pentagon. Nearly 200 more of our fellow Americans are also dead. The President told us yesterday that we are at war, and that justice will be served, that those responsible for this horrendous act against civilization itself, will be, in the President's own words, "Smoked out of their holes" and brought to account and judgment.

Symbols of American strength and security have been destroyed and severely damaged. This has been a shock beyond words. But, as we have seen in the past few days, America's resolve and patriotism have been kindled anew. And yes, millions of our citizens have turned to God for divine comfort and for hope and deliverance. Thousands have prayed for God to perform a miracle and rescue their loved ones who are trapped: pleading with an almighty providence to graciously intervene, even though hope dims with each passing hour.

I must frankly confess that I have found this entire catastrophe incomprehensible. Like most of you, I have shed tears. How can one not weep at the sight of husbands

First Sunday

and wives, of fathers and mothers, of brothers and sisters and friends, recounting the cell phone conversations with those who mattered the most to them on this earth -- some saying their last good-byes, professing their undying love in their dying hour? It has been a sadness impossible to identify with.

We come together as a church family -- as brothers and sisters in Christ -- to encourage and comfort one another. To give thanks for the safety of our families. To mourn those who have been lost. And to pray for those whose grief is too much to bear. We come also to remember our leaders, and to lift them up to God's throne of grace and to say a prayer for our beloved nation, for never before has she had to endure a calamity of such devastating magnitude.

We come here also to seek answers to the unanswerable, to make some sense of this senseless national tragedy. Our hearts are heavy. Our minds are startled and even confused. Again, as in tragic times before, we ask "Where is God?" Has He no power to stop evil? Why does He, if He is truly a God of love and justice, permit such horrible things to happen to good and innocent people? If He is a God of infinite power, why does He do nothing when bad people, filled with evil and hate, successfully execute an elaborate and well-planned attack that kills thousands and seriously wounds the world's beacon of democracy and freedom? Why is it that we are so often forced to look upon, in the words of James Russell Lowell, "Truth forever on the scaffold, wrong forever on the throne...?"

How can a just and all powerful and holy God allow the triumph of evil? We are saddened and hurt when bad things happen to good people. But we are troubled, mystified and yes, angry, when good things happen to bad people; when we see our fellow citizens crying for their families buried alive last Tuesday, while the supporters of those who did this to us celebrate in the streets, handing out candy.

Doubts. Yes, let's admit it: this incomprehensible tragedy has created doubts. And questions. Many questions.

A long time ago, a man named Asaph had similar doubts. He could not understand why God permitted the wicked to do so well, to accomplish so much. The triumph of the wicked flew directly into the face of God's supposed omnipotence and justice. Asaph couldn't figure it out. It simply didn't add up.

As we turn to the 73rd Psalm, we see in the psalmist's perplexity our own doubts and incomprehension about the ways of God and the way of evil in the world. We see also the psalmist's choice -- and a similar choice that you and I have to make in the face of a reality which cannot be explained. And so too, as the psalmist concludes this 73rd

First Sunday

Psalm with an expression of his hope, we are invited to anchor our own confidence in the midst of uncertainty.

The Psalmist's Perplexity And Ours.

Asaph says in verse 12, "This is what the wicked are like." And he has, in fact, described them previously: arrogant, successful, without regard for God, "always carefree," that is, always committing sin with impunity. He says that his own attempts at goodness, at living righteously are "in vain." He says it not once but twice. In verse 14 he writes, "All day long I have been plagued; I have been punished every morning."

On Tuesday morning, the wicked delivered a punishment of monumental proportions -- a plague of desolation and destruction. Among the dead are undoubtedly those who loved God, who loved and served Jesus Christ, loved their children, were good providers, faithful spouses, servants in their church and in their community. And it may be said that those they leave behind, suddenly grieving and asking "Why?" are of the same quality of character. Of the same faith. The same devotion. Is it any wonder that the psalmist said, "But as for me, my feet had almost slipped; I had nearly lost my foothold..." (v. 2)

Ascendant evil and unexplained tragedy can -- and often do -- rock our faith. We begin to doubt. We begin to turn away. We pray and He is silent. We ask "Why?" and He gives no response. If we are totally honest with ourselves, we even begin to wonder if there is a God after all. Then we feel guilty for doubting, failing to remember that God realizes that we are, for all our professions of confidence and trust, still human. And He does not judge our human frailty, because He loves us and because He gave His Son up for us, and because He is, as the scriptures remind us in so many places, a God full of compassion, mercy and grace. No, we may not always understand God, but we may be quite certain that God always understands us.

The psalmist writes in verse 16, "When I tried to understand all this it was oppressive to me..."
What would Asaph say about what happened last Tuesday morning? Would he not cry out, with millions of Americans, "Oh my God!" Would he not stake his head sadly as he watched TV and say, "Why God? Why? Why do we have to have pain and suffering and evil? Why did you let them get away with this?"

During a television interview, together with her family, a young woman was asked what might have happened if her husband, Jeremy, who had bravely struggled with the hijackers on the plane that crashed into the Pennsylvania countryside instead of hitting the White House, had gone ahead with his plans to delay his flight. She immediately responded "I just don't want to go there." The interviewer then suggested, "It is possible that your husband may have

First Sunday

helped to save the White House." "I know," she responded, "but I just can't talk about it."

"When I tried to understand all this it was oppressive to me." It is too much to take in, to even think about.

The psalmist was perplexed -- and so too are we often confounded, shaken, amazed and emotionally "oppressed" by what we see and hear, and sometimes experience. It is beyond comprehension. It is beyond explanation. It is beyond words. It is even, on occasion, beyond our contemplation. It's just too much. And we "don't want to go there."

Not only was the psalmist perplexed, as we often are. He also faced a choice, as do we.

The Psalmist's Choice - And Ours.

In verse 17, Asaph writes that things didn't make sense "until I entered the sanctuary of God." The sanctuary of God. That's where we gain a clearer perspective. That's where we begin to form a larger context. For "in the sanctuary of God" we find God. He's waiting there patiently for us to come to Him so He can take us in His arms and hold us and hug us and tell us that He loves us. We don't need to go to a church building to find God, of course, although thousands of Americans attended church services all across the country on Friday. People from all walks of life, all faith traditions and religious practices, united in a desire to seek an eternal perspective; a divine framework within which they could place a national tragedy.

Who knows what they all believe about religion and God. Not the same thing, undoubtedly. But still, it is amazing how a national crisis binds our nation together, not just politically, but, in a strange sort of way, spiritually. People seeking after God, which they are created to do - in the awareness of their own, and even their powerful country's, sudden vulnerability. Asaph chose to go to the sanctuary to find understanding; he sought the wisdom that God has promised to those who ask Him for it. Acknowledging his own weakness and limitations, he prayed and asked God to help him, to give him strength - to grant him wisdom, courage, peace, and even joy.

You and I have that same choice. We can go our own way and try to figure everything out apart from God. We can suppose that we really are, in our puny human strength, sufficient for these things. But even as the towers of the World Trade Center could not withstand the impact of a 767 jet loaded with fuel, neither can you make sense, obtain strength, get wisdom or find meaning in life apart from God. It is not possible.

"Then," says Asaph, "I understood their final destiny" (v. 17) Whose final destiny? The wicked. You see, the

First Sunday

hijackers only thought their mission had been accomplished, but the American giant has been aroused in a mighty and righteous anger. God may yet choose our nation as His appointed instrument to pour out His wrath upon these radical terrorists and their suppliers. But regardless of what happens -- whether or not there is war -- God is still on His glorious throne. He rules, proclaims the book of Revelation, as "King of the flood forever." The Pentagon may be bombed and burning, the World Trade Center may lay in ruins, but the Almighty Creator and Ruler of the universe -- the King of kings and Lord of lords -- has not been caught off guard by this attack. His divine arm has not been slackened, His glory has not been tarnished or dimmed, nor His power wounded or diminished in any way. He is now, and will be in all of eternity, our great, triumphant, victorious God!

So these hijackers did not, in fact, reach their final destination when they hit their intended targets. But they surely will. They surely will.

And our choice to choose God and His sanctuary will help us to also remain loving, even as we seek justice. Let us remember, as followers of Jesus Christ, that the entire Arab population did not commit this atrocity. When we enter into the presence of God, when we seek His face and His wisdom, we understand that the heart of humankind is, as Jeremiah tells us, "Deceitful above all things, and desperately wicked, who can know it?' And when we go to

His sanctuary, when we come honestly before Him, we also understand that this human depravity includes us all. C. S. Lewis was right: "We are fallen creatures living in a fallen world."

And yet, in the wake of this disaster, the incredible displays of courage, heroism, kindness, compassion and generosity by our fellow citizens, remind us that we are, even in this fallen condition of humanity, created in God's divine image. His unmistakable Imago Dei is stamped indelibly on every human heart, no matter how desperately and despicably we may sometimes behave. To God we are nonetheless redeemable. Let's not forget that and, as difficult as it is in this case, let us find a place for forgiveness, for we have been forgiven much.

So let us seek justice but leave vengeance and eternal judgment to our God Who is, as the psalmist reminds us, "Altogether just." Let us seek Him and "we shall surely find Him, though He be not far from every one of us." Let us, like the psalmist, choose to know God in His sanctuary. And He will grant us wisdom and true understanding. And courage to face a tomorrow that is very uncertain.

The psalmist faced perplexity, and so do we. The psalmist had a choice and so, too, do we. The psalmist found a hope.... And so can we.

First Sunday

The Psalmist's Hope - And Ours

In verses 21 and 22, Asaph describes his situation -- and his emotions -- with words that ring true in our own hearts: "my heart was grieved and my spirit embittered; I was senseless and ignorant." That sounds like a lot of Americans this past week -- including many Christians. Grief-stricken and bitter, angry, resentful, bent on revenge. But the psalmist moves quickly, in the closing verses of this profound expression of his experience, to proclaim his hope in God, Who is - for Asaph and for you and me - an ultimate hope, an eternal hope, our true hope. In verse 23 he writes, "Yet I am always with you; you hold me by my right hand."

God is always with us, so we may dwell and abide always with Him and with His Son, our Lord and Savior Jesus Christ. He has promised never to leave us, no matter what. And in every situation, He has promised us His strength and His grace to take us through. He will do that for the thousands of grieving Americans who place their faith and hope in Him. He will do the same for you and for me.

"Those who fully trust Him find Him fully true."

God wants to take us by the hand and lead us through whatever it is we may have to face. God can do anything, except fail us. He is faithful, Paul told Timothy, even when we have no faith left. He is our strength when we are weak. Our comfort when we are sad. Our refuge when we are frightened.

Thousands fled the twin towers -- and thousands did not make it out in time. Once thought impregnable, they toppled like Legos. But Proverbs tells us: "The name of the Lord is a strong tower; the righteous run to it and are safe." (Proverbs 18:10)

In verse 25, the now praising Asaph says, "Whom have I in heaven but you?" Then he says this: "in being with you I desire nothing on earth." You see, my friends, God is all you and I need. And He will meet, He will provide, all our needs. He will give us what we need in this hour of trial. For even in the darkest hour; even through the longest night; even under the most desperate and ominous of circumstances, whether those be personal or national, He is the God Who is there -- and He is not silent.

Listen to His still, small voice whisper to your heart, and speak "peace, be still" to your mind. "I'm here," He says. "I know you need me, and you have me. I am with you. I will guide you and afterward take you into my glory and my heavenly kingdom. You are mine. My only Son purchased your redemption with His own blood, so you know that I love you. Take my hand; we'll go through this together."

"My flesh and my heart may fail," concedes the psalmist in verse 26. After all, we are in the final analysis only

First Sunday

mortals. "But God is the strength of my heart and my portion forever."

In this our hour of great national despair, when our hearts may fail us and our human strength be insufficient, God -- and God alone -- is our hope. Harry Emerson Fosdick, who was the longtime pastor of the Riverside Church in New York City, once wrote a hymn entitled "God of Grace and God of Glory." It is appropriate that on this occasion we close this message with the words of that great hymn:

God of grace and God of glory, on Thy people pour Thy power; Crown Thine ancient Church's story; Bring her bud to glorious flower. Grant us wisdom, grant us courage, For the facing of this hour, for the facing of this hour. Lo! The hosts of evil round us, scorn Thy Christ, assail His ways! From the fears that long have bound us, free our hearts to faith and praise. Grant us wisdom, grant us courage, For the living of these days, for the living of these days. Cure Thy children's warring madness, bend our pride to Thy control; Shame our wanton, selfish gladness, rich in things and poor in soul. Grant us wisdom, grant us courage, Lest we miss Thy kingdom's goal, lest we miss Thy kingdom's goal. Set our feet on lofty places; Gird our lives that they may be Armored with all Christlike graces in the fight to set men free. Grant us wisdom, grant us courage, That we fail not man nor Thee, that we fail not man nor Thee.

Donald Robert Elton & Aura Agudo Elton

About the Editors

Aura Agudo Elton was born in The Republic of Panama and completed law school at the University of Panama and moved to the United States September 8, 2001, just in time to witness the 9-11 attacks. She has a Masters degree from Winthrop University. She is a university Spanish instructor and medical office manager. She is interested in politics, education, and immigration. She has been a board member in the United Way and was a cofounder of the International Center of York County (ICYC) in Rock Hill, SC.

Donald Robert Elton was born in California. He completed his undergraduate education at the University of South Carolina and completed medical school at the Medical University of South Carolina. He is a board certified pulmonary medicine specialist practicing in the Columbia, SC, area. He is a private pilot and is interested in politics, medical education, as well as North, Central, and South American History.

Email: delton@lexpcc.net

Website: http://FirstSundayBook.com
(contains latest information about how to order additional copies of the book in paperback and eBook formats)

Made in the USA
Charleston, SC
21 February 2011